YA Programs

Hip-Hop Symposiums, Summer Reading Programs, Virtual Tours, Poetry Slams, Teen Advisory Boards, Term Paper Clinics, and More!

Ella W. Jones

Neal-Schuman Publishers, Inc.

New York   London

Published by Neal-Schuman Publishers, Inc.
100 William St., Suite 2004
New York, NY 10038

Printed and bound in the United States of America.

The paper used in this publication meets the minimum requirements of American National Standard for Information Sciences-Permanence of Paper for Printed Library Materials, ANSI Z39.48-1992.

Library of Congress Cataloging-in-Publication Data

Jones, Ella W.
    Start-to-finish YA programs : hip-hop symposiums, summer reading programs, virtual tours, poetry slams, teen advisory boards, term paper clinics, and more! / Ella W. Jones.
        p. cm.
    Includes bibliographical references and index.
    ISBN 978-1-55570-601-2 (alk. paper)
    1. Young adults' libraries—Activity programs. 2. Libraries and teenagers. I. Title.

Z718.5.J65 2009
027.62'6—dc22
                                                                    2008050853

CONTENTS

LIST OF FIGURES

FOREWORD

One of the best parts of providing training for library staff members on services to teens is how much I learn. For example, the third edition of *Connecting Young Adults and Libraries* (Neal-Schuman, 2004) is loaded with best practices I've picked up presenting workshops across the United States and Canada. It is amazing the great work happening with teens in school and public libraries and how eager people are to share that information with their colleagues during workshops. The hardest part of these workshops is ending the "best practices" sharing segment because often people have so much to share. I often suggest people consider writing articles for the professional literature when I hear about a particularly strong or unique program.

When I presented a workshop in Arlington, Texas, in April 2005, I realized that one person in the audience had enough materials for a book, not just an article. Ella totally blew away all of us at that workshop with her ideas, her experiences, and her enthusiasm for teen programming. I suggested she consider a book for Neal-Schuman on the topic of teen programming, with a focus on urban libraries. Within a few weeks, she had an outline ready and a good part of the book pulled together from her work at the Fort Worth Public Library.

What Ella brings to the table isn't just her experience as a librarian, but years of work with teens as a teacher—an award-winning teacher. But more than that, Ella brings an urban experience into this field of young adult programming. Ella's background brings to the forefront the important role that librarians can play in the lives of inner-city teens.

That is, you do the right program for the right audience at the right time. Ella's not just looking at planning and promoting programs, but rather at the bigger picture of marketing. That formula of the six Ps (plus one!) grounds librarians in perhaps the hardest, yet most essential element of presenting successful teen programs. It's not about flyers or posters, but figuring out what you are selling, to whom you are selling it, and how you plan to get teens to "buy" your program. So, in addition to marketing, Ella gives us reminders (or new info for many) on how to sell.

Yet, this book isn't just about the sizzle; it's about the steak—steak that she's cooked and served for you in 25 program packets. What I've tried to do in all three editions of *Connecting Young Adults and Libraries* is make the information contained therein practical, but Ella's gone a step better. The information is not only practical; it's ready to use. Given busy schedules, less people to do this work, and more demands on our time, Ella provides all of us with 25 turnkey teen programs. This is how-to-do-it taken to a whole new level of detail, perfect for beginners but still useful for the seasoned programming professional.

Both beginners and experienced librarians, however, know that, above all else, the most important element to consider in planning any service, any program, any collection, or any new initiative is to know the audience you want to reach. Ella's background in urban libraries provides a foundation for the work here to reach that audience, but the ideas and energy can work wherever staff seek to connect young adults and libraries.

Patrick Jones
Young Adult Services Consultant
and Award-winning Author
www.connectingya.com

PREFACE

The episode of the *Oprah Winfrey Show* that aired on October 26, 2005, concerned addictions. At the end of the program, Oprah announced that, because she was so impressed with the author of the book she had featured on her program that day, she was going to make a donation to the ALA (American Library Association) to help fund teen programs. She explained that having more programs available for teens would help prevent many of them from taking the path her guest author had chosen as a teen.

Oprah's statement—that library programs for teens can prevent problems—reinforces what young adult (YA) librarians already know and what the Search Institute®'s 40 Developmental Assets® assert: Programs designed to serve teens will help them grow up to be healthy, caring, and responsible adults. This belief is also behind my personal motto: *If we can reach one, we can teach one.* YA programs do just that.

My daughter saw Oprah's show that day. Afterward, she called me. She was very excited and said, "Mom, society needs your book!" I had already started writing my book, but this re-inspired me. It gave me the validation that I needed to share these valuable resources.

To assess what to convey in a book on YA programming, I conducted telephone interviews with teen librarians and library assistants, whom I selected from the Fort Worth Public Library System and surrounding cities to ensure inclusion of users of all types of libraries. Ninety-five percent of those polled felt a need for a workbook on teen programming. Creative ideas and how to plan the event were the participants' greatest concerns.

CONTENT

Start-to-Finish YA Programs both showcases and is a planning tool for creative and innovative methods of developing programs for teenagers. Part I, "Let's Get Started!," discusses why we should provide programs for teens and describes how to plan, market, and evaluate the programs. To help librarians apply for grants, the Search Institute's 40 Developmental Assets are included along with a companion list of programs supporting each group of assets. Part II, "Twenty-Five Creative and Innovative Teen Programs," showcases 25 teen-tested programs, with customizable flyers, rave cards, registration forms, sign-up sheets, and more, as well as a few PowerPoint presentations, all of which are included on the accompanying CD-ROM. Program packets also include step-by-step instructions on how to produce the programs start to finish: from initial planning to publicity, to conducting and evaluating the program. Explaining the goals of the programs, including the Developmental Assets the programs address, is invaluable when presenting a program idea to library administrators. The programs cover a variety of interests: music, fashion, dance, business, competition, and literature. Part III, "The Finish Line," discusses the outcome of programming for teens, includes a grant-writing resource list, and provides additional resources and references.

THE NEED FOR PROGRAMMING RESOURCES

I spent over 25 years in the field of education (15 years as a high school teacher, 5 years as a counselor/acting assistant principal of an alterative high school, and 7 years as the director of a private elementary school) before switching to librarianship. I first got the idea to write a book to provide guidelines on planning and implementing library programs for teenagers when I was working on the thesis for my master's degree in library and information science at the University of North Texas (UNT), called the Capstone Experience. I had many discussions about teen programming with practicing young adult librarians and members of the Texas Library Association (TLA). I have also conducted discussion workshops for North Texas Regional Library Systems (NTRLS) titled "Can We Talk . . . About Teen Programming" and "Can We Talk a Little Close . . . Teen Programming for Small/ Rural Libraries."

The discussions about teen programming always included comments like "the need for useful tools and sources," as well as "meeting teens' developmental needs." Teen librarians frequently mentioned that separating young adult library users from adult or children users is a relatively recent development in libraries. Therefore, many library schools do not instruct librarians on the information they need to develop teen programs by giving them practical how-to instructions, strategies, and tools.

There are similarities between education and librarianship: providing information, guidance, and instruction to students and other library users such as parents, teachers, and school administrators. Librarians who learn how to do effective teen programming will increase library usage as well as meet teens' developmental needs. By sponsoring programs for young adults, the library community is more likely to retain teenagers as library users who will become library supporters as adults. Libraries do not, should not, and cannot develop services and programs for young adults because it is good *only* for the library, but rather because these services and programs will make an affirmative impact leading to positive outcomes for teens. "Healthy youth create healthy communities in which libraries can thrive" (Jones, 2002: 16).

This resource book with accompanying CD-ROM was designed for libraries, schools, youth groups—anyone who works with teens. According to Department of Education statistics, public high school enrollment is expected to continue to increase, which will have a great impact on all types of organizations that serve young adults, ages 13 through 19. The need for more trained caregivers is obvious. It makes no difference if the organization is a library, a school, a church, or a youth club—all will feel the impact of the greater numbers in this client group now and in the years to come. Be prepared with Start-to-Finish YA Programs.

REFERENCE

Jones, Patrick. 2002. *New Directions for Library Service to Young Adults*. Chicago: American Library Association.

ACKNOWLEDGMENTS

I would like to thank Divetta "D" Metcalf, my fellow coworker, for persuading me in her special way to write this book. Thanks to my lovely daughter, Raquel Jones, who has always been the inspiration of my life, for encouraging me to stay focused. Thanks also to Jackie Spinks, one of my closest friends and business partners, for staying on me to finish. Thank you to Attorney Stacy Dunlop for his legal assistance. Thanks to my two nieces Janay Windom and Keyana Jones along with my nephew Tayo Ojo for allowing me to use their pictures for the Teen Top Models Fashion Course—they had a lot to do with inspiring me to create that program. Thanks to my family, especially my two sisters, Erma Jones and Selma Windom, along with my brother-in-law Carl Windom and my big brother Melvin Jones Jr.—they have forever been supportive of my efforts. Thank you to my cousin Rene Hightire for constantly checking on me to see how I was coming along. (Good luck on your book.) And last but not least, thanks to Ursula Brockman, Gladys Brown, Karen Mims, and Dean Washington for their believing I could do it and for being my friends—and because if I had not mentioned their names they would never let me live it down.

To RoseMary Honnold, I can't thank you enough for all of your help.

PART I

LET'S GET STARTED!

WHY OFFER PROGRAMS FOR TEENS?

Teens have strong needs to socialize, and their gathering place options have become increasingly limited. These gathering places are important for the health of communities. To fill this void, teens are joining various online social networking sites such as MySpace and Facebook. Some teens say the online environment is more hospitable than many libraries. In light of this trend, libraries can contribute to the health of their communities by providing teens with programs that give them a place and an opportunity to gather. Teens are the next generation of library users, and we will lose them if we don't make them feel that they are a part of their community.

It is a universal challenge to think of new ways to attract teens into the library, especially given the competition of the Internet. The question library staff ask most is, "How do we get teens into the library?" Common follow-up questions are, "What do we do with them once we get them here?" and "How do we get them to use the library as we want them to, rather than however they choose?" In other words, most librarians think of teen users as a problem. Some studies indicate that teens represent almost 25 percent of public library users, so they should not be viewed as problems to solve but rather as customers to be served.

Most research suggests that the top three reasons teens use public libraries are to do research, to volunteer, and to use the Internet (Loertscher and Woolls, 2002; Bishop and Bauer, 2002). Because public library attendance is not compulsory, as with school attendance, this creates a challenge for librarians: to select the best means of attracting the attention of teens to have the opportunity to develop and strengthen their information literacy. Awareness of young adults as library users has risen dramatically over the past decade:

> The Public Library Association's (PLA) 2007 Public Library Data Service (PLDS) Statistical Report tracked young adult service trends in public libraries. The report found that nearly 90 percent of the public libraries surveyed offer young adult programs, with more than half (51.9 percent) employing at least one full-time equivalent dedicated to fostering young adult programs and services, up dramatically from 11 percent in 1995. (American Library Association, 2007)

The key to keeping teens in our libraries is to continually involve them in library activities and programs.

Libraries are no longer the place where librarians consistently shush patrons. A growing trend of libraries around the country is to become centers of activity, organized with the intention of attracting those who are otherwise not using them. The way to get teens in is to create specialized programming that will get their attention. The good news is that some public libraries are now overflowing with teens. During the past ten years, these teens have suddenly found the library to be a place that encourages independence, learning, socialization, and creativity. The bad news is that the majority of teens still do not visit libraries. Still, I truly believe more young people would use libraries if they understood their true value. The solution is to initiate a major paradigm shift by making reaching out to teens a priority.

According to a study cited by Gross (2001), fulfilling school assignments is the reason why most teens use the public library. Teens know they can come to the library to work on homework and to do research. Still there is a need for positive marketing to create other reasons for teens to become patrons. We must let them know that the library is also the place where they can come for recreation and socialization.

To reach teens we must try to understand where they are coming from. The current status of teens in society, according to Jami Jones (2004), is that half of all teens have been affected by the divorce of their parents, one in five lives in poverty, and approximately one in six suffers from depression. Thirty-five percent of girls get pregnant at least once before age 20. Therefore, in addition to just providing access to technology and to a "safe" place to be during out-of-school hours, libraries can provide youth programs to help teens cope with the stresses in their lives and also improve their personal and social skills. According to "New on the Shelf: Teens in the Library—Findings from the Evaluation of Public Libraries as Partners in Youth Development" (Spielberger et al., 2005), to work with teens calls for an alignment of youth programs with the library's core mission and goals. It also requires time, resources, a dedicated staff, and consistent leadership. New and innovative programs can have positive impacts on the library system as well as on the community (Spielberger et al., 2005).

The reasons for working with teens can be divided into two categories: reactive and proactive. For years librarians have mostly ignored young adults, much of the time as a reaction of fear. Fear, in the world of libraries, usually stems from the presence of homeless people, teenagers, and gangs (the latter two often being considered as one group). Teens are seen as unruly, unworthy, and downright dangerous (Casey, 2007). This attitude tends to scare staff, customers, and the politicians who fund libraries. Today's teenagers are tomorrow's taxpayers and library users; hence, we, as caretakers of our future, must play a proactive role by creating programs of interest that will get their attention.

One of the major obstacles to creating a teen-friendly library is the inadequate number of library staff designated to serve this population. A survey by the National Center for Education Statistics found that "only thirty percent of all public librarians who provide services directly to the public specialize in services to youth, a ratio of about one youth specialist to every 618 young people" (Chelton, 1997). This lack of specialization in a population that makes up 25 percent of library users does not seem likely to change in the near future, especially considering the budget constraints of public libraries (Egan, 2003). This book will be able to help further reduce the "specialization" obstacle. Far too often, people are so eager to get a new program started that they end up skipping some important considerations. This is likely one of the reasons that many programs fail. This manual will help ensure that your organization is really ready from *start to finish*.

THE 40 DEVELOPMENTAL ASSETS

Since 1989, the Search Institute® has surveyed more than two million sixth to twelfth graders across the United States and Canada. The study is based on the 40 Developmental Assets® that all young people need to grow up to be healthy, caring, and responsible adults.

Research has revealed a strong and consistent relationship between the degree to which young people develop in positive and healthful ways and the number of assets present in their lives. The greater the number of Developmental Assets that young people experience, the more positive and successful they will be. The fewer the number of Developmental Assets present in their lives, the greater the possibility that youth will become involved in risky behaviors and make bad choices.

The outcome of the Search Institute's studies is that the average young person surveyed in the United States experiences less than half of the 40 assets. In other words, most of the young people in this country lack an adequate number of the Developmental Assets needed to develop healthfully. Therefore, as a community we must rally to rebuild the solid foundation that many young people lack. We can nurture the positive development of youth by providing programs designed specifically to meet their needs.

A survey taken in Fort Worth, Texas, found "Reading for Pleasure" to have the lowest asset percentage reported by youth. With this information in mind, the Teen Unit of the Fort Worth Public Library strives to find ways to get more young people actively involved with the library, in turn helping to reduce the high school drop-out rate. The city, the school district, and the public library work together to help teenagers develop the 40 Developmental Assets (Figure I.1) that help young people grow up healthy, caring, and responsible.

HOW TO PLAN PROGRAMS

To instill a sense of history and culture, to educate and nurture individual and collective self-esteem, and to foster pride of culture and community, we must get young people to read. The objective of this book is to show how to implement programs to reach teens that will get them more actively involved in the library. As the caretakers of the future, librarians have a responsibility to reach out to all young people by passing knowledge on through books. But before you can *teach one, you must first reach one*, and you can reach teens best through programs. By getting young people more actively involved in the library, you can help them to be successful in school and eventually in the workplace.

It is estimated that by the year 2010 there will be more teenagers in the country than ever before (Aronson, 2002). In *New Directions for Library Services to Young Adults*, Jones (2002: 3) asked the question, "Clearly, public libraries will be looking at increased demands for their services by teenagers, but are the libraries ready for this age wave?"

Planning programs for young adults begins with creative ideas. Creative ideas begin with positive thoughts.

Practice Looking for the Positive

Nothing in life lacks meaning. Try this experiment: Look around the room and notice everything that is red. Now close your eyes and picture the room in your mind, and recall all the red things. That was not difficult. Now close your eyes again. Picture the room in your mind again. This time recall all the brown things in the room. Then open your eyes and look at the space around you. You most likely see many brown things that you did not see in your mind. You were not paying attention to brown things.

In planning for teens you must notice what you see. You may discover that you see mostly negative things about teens. A way to guide yourself away from this mindset is to decide what you will look for and to practice it. If you deliberately look for and notice positive, attractive aspects of teenagers, it will become habitual.

Figure I.1. 40 Developmental Assets® Chart

Through extensive research, Search Institute® has identified the following 40 building blocks of development that help young people grow up healthy, caring, and responsible. The asset definitions shown in this chart are based on research with adolescents (grades 6 to 12).

Asset Type	Asset Name	Asset Definition
External assets		
Support	Family support	Family life provides high levels of love and support.
	Positive family communication	Young person and her or his parent(s) communicate positively, and young person is willing to seek advice and counsel from parent(s).
	Other adult relationships	Young person receives support from three or more nonparent adults.
	Caring neighborhood	Young person experiences caring neighbors.
	Caring school climate	School provides a caring, encouraging environment.
	Parent involvement in schooling	Parent(s) are actively involved in helping young person succeed in school.
Empowerment	Community values youth	Young person perceives that adults in the community value youth.
	Youth as resources	Young people are given useful roles in the community.
	Service to others	Young person serves in the community one hour or more per week.
	Safety	Young person feels safe at home, at school, and in the neighborhood.
Boundaries and expectations	Family boundaries	Family has clear rules and consequences and monitors the young person's whereabouts.
	School boundaries	School provides clear rules and consequences
	Neighborhood boundaries	Neighbors take responsibility for monitoring young people's behavior

(Cont'd.)

Figure I.1. 40 Developmental Assets® Chart *(Continued)*

Asset Type	Asset Name	Asset Definition
Boundaries and expectations *(Cont'd.)*	Adult role models	Parent(s) and other adult model positive, responsible behavior.
	Positive peer influence	Young person's best friends model responsible behavior.
	High expectations	Both parent(s) and teachers encourage the young person to do well.
Constructive use of time	Creative activities	Young person spends three or more hours per week in lessons or practice in music, theater, or other arts.
	Youth programs	Young person spends three or more hours per week in sports, clubs, or organizations at school and/or in community organizations.
	Religious community	Young person spends one hour or more per week in activities in a religious institution.
	Time at home	Young person is out with friends "with nothing special to do" two or fewer nights per week.
Internal assets		
Commitment to learning	Achievement motivation	Young person is motivated to do well in school.
	School engagement	Young person is actively engaged in learning.
	Homework	Young person reports doing at least one hour of homework every school day.
	Bonding to school	Young person cares about her or his school.
	Reading for pleasure	Young person reads for pleasure three or more hours per week.
Positive values	Caring	Young person places high value on helping other people.
	Equality and social justice	Young person places high value on promoting equality and reducing hunger and poverty.

(Cont'd.)

Figure I.1. 40 Developmental Assets® Chart *(Continued)*

Asset Type	Asset Name	Asset Definition
Positive values *(Cont'd.)*	Integrity	Young person acts on convictions and stands up for her or his beliefs
	Honesty	Young person "tells the truth even when it is not easy."
	Responsibility	Young person accepts and takes personal responsibility.
	Restraint	Young person believes it is important not to be sexually active or to use alcohol or other drugs.
Social competencies	Planning and decision making	Young person knows how to plan ahead and make choices.
	Interpersonal competence	Young person has empathy, sensitivity, and friendship skills.
	Cultural competence	Young person has knowledge of and comfort with people of different cultural/racial/ethnic backgrounds.
	Resistance skills	Young person can resist negative peer pressure and dangerous situations.
	Peaceful conflict resolution	Young person seeks to resolve conflict nonviolently.
Positive identity	Personal power	Young person feels he or she has control over "things that happen to me."
	Self-esteem	Young person reports having a high self-esteem.
	Sense of purpose	Young person reports that "my life has a purpose."
	Positive view of personal future	Young person is optimistic about her or his personal future.

This list is an educational tool. It is not intended to be nor is it appropriate as a scientific measure of the developmental assets of individuals.

Source: The list of 40 Developmental Assets® is reprinted with permission from Search Institute®. Copyright © 1997, 2006 Search Institute, 615 First Avenue NE, Suite 125, Minneapolis, MN 55413; 800-888-7828; www.search-institute.org. The list may be reproduced for educational, noncommercial uses only. All rights reserved. The following are registered trademarks of Search Institute: Search Institute®, Developmental Assets®, and Healthy Communities • Healthy Youth®.

Creative Programs That Match Needs and Support Healthy Youth Development

The program packets included in this book are developed to help teens build assets. Browse the following lists to see which assets the programs target.

Assets #1–6: SUPPORT Them with Love, Care, and Attention

- Old School Takes New School Back to School Party
- C.L.A.S.S.: Connecting Libraries and Schools Simultaneously
- Makeup, Massage, and a Message: A Mother–Daughter Day Out
- Teen Talent Incubator
- Term Paper Clinic
- Brown Bag Concerts @ the Library
- Caravan of Jazz @ the Library
- Book Club & Jam Session @ the Library
- Youth Gospel Fest
- Hip-Hop Symposium
- Library Teen Idol Competition
- Poetry Slam
- Teen Advisory Board
- Youth Leadership Conference
- Commitment to Fitness
- Family Affair—Oral History Project
- Mission Possible: Spy a Book
- Check It Out @ the Library (Teen Cable Show)
- Word-Up (Radio Program)

Assets #7–10: EMPOWER Them with Opportunities to Make a Difference in Their Family and Community

- Brown Bag Concerts @ the Library
- Family Affair—Oral History Project
- Teen Talent Incubator
- Youth Gospel Fest
- Teen Top Models Fashion Course
- Caravan of Jazz @ the Library
- Hip-Hop Symposium
- Teen Advisory Board
- Youth Leadership Conference
- C.L.A.S.S.: Connecting Libraries and Schools Simultaneously
- Check It Out @ the Library (Teen Cable Show)
- Word-Up (Radio Program)

Assets #11–16: Establish Clear BOUNDARIES and Have High EXPECTATIONS

- Library Teen Idol Competition
- Teen Talent Incubator
- Poetry Workshop
- Teen Top Models Fashion Course
- Caravan of Jazz @ the Library
- Book Club & Jam Session @ the Library
- Hip-Hop Symposium
- Poetry Slam
- Teen Advisory Board
- Youth Leadership Conference
- C.L.A.S.S.: Connecting Libraries and Schools Simultaneously
- Check It Out @ the Library (Teen Cable Show)
- Makeup, Massage, and a Message: A Mother–Daughter Day Out

(Cont'd.)

Assets #17–20: Help Them Find Activities That Make CONSTRUCTIVE USE of Their TIME

- Poetry Workshop
- Poetry Slam
- DJ Workshop—Who Wants to Be a DJ?
- Minding Your Own Business Seminar
- Teen Top Models Fashion Course
- Brown Bag Concerts @ the Library
- Youth Gospel Fest
- Library Teen Idol Competition
- Teen Advisory Board
- Commitment to Fitness
- Family Affair—Oral History Project
- Check It Out @ the Library (Teen Cable Show)
- Word-Up (Radio Program)

Assets #21–25: Nurture in Them a COMMITMENT TO LEARNING

- Term Paper Clinic
- Homework Seminar
- Mission Possible: Spy a Book
- Poetry Workshop
- Teen Talent Incubator
- Teen Top Models Fashion Course
- Caravan of Jazz @ the Library
- Book Club & Jam Session @ the Library
- Hip-Hop Symposium
- Poetry Slam
- Teen Advisory Board
- Youth Leadership Conference
- C.L.A.S.S.: Connecting Libraries and Schools Simultaneously
- Old School Takes New School Back to School Party

Assets #26–31: Instill POSITIVE VALUES to Guide Them

- Teen Advisory Board
- Commitment to Fitness
- DJ Workshop—Who Wants to Be a DJ?
- Poetry Workshop
- Hip-Hop Symposium
- Poetry Slam
- Youth Leadership Conference
- Check It Out @ the Library (Teen Cable Show)

Assets #32–36: Help Them Develop Life Skills and SOCIAL COMPETENCIES

- Youth Leadership Conference
- Book Club & Jam Session @ the Library
- DJ Workshop—Who Wants to Be a DJ?
- Poetry Workshop
- Teen Talent Incubator
- Caravan of Jazz @ the Library
- Youth Gospel Fest
- Hip-Hop Symposium
- Poetry Slam
- Teen Advisory Board
- Commitment to Fitness
- Family Affair—Oral History Project
- Check It Out @ the Library (Teen Cable Show)

Assets #37–40: Nurture, Celebrate, and Affirm Their POSITIVE IDENTITY

- Hip-Hop Symposium
- Check It Out @ the Library (Teen Cable Show)
- Minding Your Own Business Seminar
- DJ Workshop—Who Wants to Be a DJ?
- Poetry Workshop
- Teen Talent Incubator
- Teen Top Models Fashion Course
- Brown Bag Concerts @ the Library
- Youth Gospel Fest
- Library Teen Idol Competition
- Poetry Slam
- Teen Advisory Board
- Youth Leadership Conference
- Commitment to Fitness
- Check It Out @ the Library (Teen Cable Show)

Brainstorming Creative Ideas for Teen Programming

Program ideas come from many places. They come from reading articles and books, watching TV, talking to people about their professional development needs, and studying what others are doing (Simerly, 1990). Needless to say, not every idea will be marketable.

SWOT Analysis

Begin planning your programs by performing a SWOT analysis in which you analyze your library's strengths, weaknesses, opportunities, and threats (see Figure I.2). Consider the following example.

- **S**trengths the library has to offer teens: Libraries offer a safe haven for teens, free from gang violence. The programs are usually educational in nature and are offered for free. Libraries have the resources to satisfy the curious nature of young people. Many libraries have the facilities to host forums such as Hip-Hop Symposiums.
- **W**eaknesses that may exist: Teens have very busy schedules. Library programming must compete with school extracurricular activities. In many situations teens see the library as an extension of school—someplace they don't want to be if they don't have to. Often teachers and parents are also unaware of the resources available to students in the library. Young people do what they see adults do. If they do not see their parents using the library, then chances are they too will not become users.
- **O**pportunities that may come from the weaknesses: Although most high school students have very little time to attend library functions, homeschoolers are looking for something to do. Establish a relationship with other organizations that serve young people, such as the YMCA, the YWCA, and the Boys & Girls Clubs of America. These organizations are looking for activities for their teen population. Fortunately, they often have vans or buses for transportation. They are just looking for some place to go.
- **T**hreats that may possibly affect teen programming in the future: During the summer, students take jobs and also go on extended family vacations. During the school year, many students are saturated with homework, visiting the public library only for research information, not to attend programs. As with weaknesses, there are also opportunities to be found in threats. Using the first example, summer employment, the beginning of summer would be a great time to offer a job etiquette program or a computer training course to help prepare young people for the job market. Concerning the second threat, homework saturation, this would be a great time to offer a Homework Seminar or a Term Paper Clinic. Maybe you could start with the Parent Teacher Association to show parents and teachers the significance of the programs. They in turn will encourage students to take part.

THE SIX Ps + ONE

1. **Product**—Our products are programs that serve young adults. Base the programs on the developmental needs of the teens and on the Developmental Assets. By involving young adults from beginning to end, you provide them with creative outlets and promote the use of library resources.

Figure I.2. SWOT Analysis Worksheet

Perform a SWOT analysis on your programs. For each, list your strengths, weaknesses, opportunities, and threats.

Strengths	Weaknesses

Opportunities	Threats

2. **Public**—Teens are our target audience, but we must not stop there. As Patrick Jones (2002: 6) explains, "The approach to library services for young adults also needs to be holistic and include families, teachers, and other members of the community who work to provide healthy youth development activities for young adults."

3. **Price**—The programs may be free to the public, but there is usually a cost associated for materials, services, and staff labor.

4. **Place**—Choose an adequate location to accommodate the program and its audience. Utilize meeting room space as well as lecture halls to host programs for young adults.

5. **Production**—Determine the purpose of the event and what the library is trying to achieve by establishing specific and measurable objectives that the event is intended to accomplish (Meskauskas, 1993). Match the event to the purpose it is intended to serve.

6. **Promotion**—Traditionally word of mouth is the best form of advertisement, but this is not always easy to achieve. Flyers are often used to promote teen activities. Teens also like rave cards (postcards). They are smaller than flyers and can be passed around easily. Public Service Announcements are ads in newspapers or spots on the radio or television that you do not pay for.

+1. **Partnership**—Partner with other community organizations, such as school districts, Boys & Girls Clubs, the YWCA and the YMCA, and the Chamber of Commerce.

HOW TO EVALUATE PROGRAMS

According to *Merriam-Webster's Collegiate Dictionary*, to evaluate is "to determine or fix the value of" and "to determine the significance, worth, or condition of usually by careful appraisal and study." Evaluation is important for a number of reasons: it provides budget and decision-making rationale; seeks to improve teaching and learning for enhanced performance; provides additional data for assessing performance; and gives documentation. Conceptually, four elements should be used to evaluate all or most activities: reaction, learning, behavior, and results. Additionally, there should be a general evaluation of the overall experience and items that are specific to the program (Avery, Dahlin, and Carver, 2001).

The Program Evaluation Form shown in Figure I.3 can be customized (see version on the accompanying CD) to any of the programs you design.

REFERENCES

American Library Association. 2007. "Youth and Library Use Studies Show Gains in Serving Young Adults." Press release, July 24. Available: www.ala.org/ala/newspresscenter/news/pressreleases2007/july2007/yalsastudy07.cfm (accessed November 5, 2008).

Aronson, Marc. 2002. "Coming of Age: One Editor's View of How Young Adult Publishing Developed in America." *Publishers Weekly* (February 11): 82–86.

Avery, Elizabeth Fuseler, Terry Dahlin, and Deborah A. Carver. 2001. *Staff Development: A Practical Guide*, 3rd ed. Chicago: American Library Association.

Bishop, K. and P. Bauer. 2002. "Attracting Young Adults to Public Libraries: Frances Henne/YALSA/VOYA Research Grant Results." *Journal of Youth Services in Libraries* 15, no. 2: 36–44.

Figure I.3. Program Evaluation Form

<PROGRAM TITLE>

Evaluation Form

Program Date:

The purpose of this program was: _____

Circle your responses:

Objectives:	Agree				Disagree
The hands-on activities were fun as well as educational.	5	4	3	2	1
The information was helpful.	5	4	3	2	1
Because of this experience, I am encouraged to return to the library to take advantage of its many resources.	5	4	3	2	1
This is the type of program that I would attend or participate in again.	5	4	3	2	1
	Excellent				Poor
Overall, I considered this Series to be:	5	4	3	2	1

Suggestions:

Comments:

Please check one: _____ Youth _____ Teen _____ Adult

(Optional) Name: _____

Thank you!

Casey, Michael. 2007. "Practitioners of Panic and the Culture of Fear." Posted June 6, on the blog "Service for the Next Generation Library: A Library 2.0 Perspective." Available: www.library crunch.com/2007/06/practioners_of_panic_and_the_c.html (accessed November 5, 2008).

Chelton, M.K. 1997. "Three in Five Public Library Users Are Youth." *Public Libraries* 36, no. 2, 104–108.

Egan, Noelle. 2003. "Young Adults as Library Users: A Review of the Literature" (May 29). Available: www.pages.drexel.edu/~nme26/ROL.htm (accessed November 5, 2008).

Gross, M. 2001. "Imposed Information Seeking in Public Libraries and School Library Media Centers: A Common Behavior?" *Information Research* 6, no. 2 (January): 1–25.

Jones, J. 2004. "Beyond Books: What Can We Do to Help Troubled Teens Cope?" *School Library Journal* 50, no. 1 (January): 37.

Jones, Patrick. 2002. *New Directions for Library Services to Young Adults*. Young Adult Library Services Association. Chicago: American Library Association.

Loertscher, D.B. and B. Woolls. 2002. "Teenage Users of Libraries." *Knowledge Quest* 30, no. 5: 31–36.

Meskauskas, Debora. 1993. *Powerful Public Relations: A How-To Guide for Libraries*. Chicago: American Library Association.

Simerly, Robert. 1990. *Planning and Marketing Conferences and Workshops: Tips, Tools, and Techniques*. San Francisco: Jossey-Bass.

Spielberger, Julie, Carol Horton, Lisa Michels, and Robert Halpern. 2005. "New on the Shelf: Teens in the Library—Findings from the Evaluation of Public Libraries as Partners in Youth Development." Chapin Hall Center for Children. Available: www.chapinhall .org/article_abstract.aspx?ar=1380 (accessed November 5, 2008).

PART II

TWENTY-FIVE CREATIVE AND INNOVATIVE TEEN PROGRAMS

1
DJ WORKSHOP—WHO WANTS TO BE A DJ?

PROGRAM DESCRIPTION

Who Wants to Be a DJ? is a series of disc jockey (DJ) training workshops. Teen participants are taught the business of being a DJ along with getting hands-on experience. A local DJ teaches young people DJ skills, such as how to use and respect DJ equipment, how to "spin" and "scratch" records, how to operate turntables and cross-faders, and how to use mixing and beat matching effectively. The tools and techniques of the DJ show teens how, with a little practice, they can let their creativity shine through music.

PROGRAM GOALS

Music is a part of almost every teenager's life. We hope to make the library a part of their lives also. The DJ workshop puts music and the library together, making the library a more teen-friendly place and therefore inviting teens to get more actively involved in the library. The workshop offers a way for teens to kick-start their musical creativity in an attitude-free and friendly environment, while gaining greater respect for the work of the DJ and the equipment. The program helps teens find activities that make constructive use of their time (Developmental Assets® #17–20), instill positive values to guide them (Developmental Assets #26–31), help them develop life skills and social competencies (Developmental Assets #32–36), and nurture, celebrate, and affirm their positive identity (Developmental Assets #37–40).

HOW TO DO IT

Step 1: Make a Plan

For every program, set the groundwork for success by first obtaining permission from the library administrators. In smaller libraries, this may be a ten-minute conversation with the director, but in larger library systems, the process may take a few weeks to travel through several tiers of management. Learn the approval process before discussing program ideas with your teens to avoid disappointment if the idea runs into a snag. After approval, take the idea to your teens. Brainstorm with your Teen Advisory Board or with teens who hang around the library. Ask them what they would like to learn in the workshop and ask them to sign up to help with advertising, setup, and cleanup. They may also be able to suggest DJs for the job.

Fees to hire the DJ will vary from community to community. Our DJ cost was $75.00 per session. If the cost does not fit into your programming budget, consider writing a grant or requesting funds from a local civic club that supports teen activities.

Step 2: Set a Date, Book a Space

The workshops are one-hour sessions once a month. Your budget will help you determine how many sessions you will have in your series, as well as the availability of your DJ. Our library held six workshops at a cost of $450.00.

You need an appropriate location for a noise-intensive program. Most large library systems have a teen area that can accommodate relatively noisy programs, such as movies or video games; however, the DJ workshops are especially noisy. You will want to allow teens to experiment with volume and bass levels that might disturb other patrons, so you will want to stage the program in a noise-insulated area like an auditorium. If such an area is not available, the program should be scheduled when the library is closed or at a low-traffic time and as far from the main area of the library as possible. If the program takes place during regular hours, a large meeting room or a room on another floor may be the best choice. At Fort Worth Public Library, the classes were held in the Teen Center "Our Place" in the Central Library.

Step 3: Book the Presenter

Ideally, you want a professional DJ who will bring his or her own equipment and music to facilitate the workshops. Ask your teens if they know any DJs who have worked local school dances. Ask your fellow staff members, who may know DJs from local entertainment establishments or wedding receptions. Recommended DJs are your best options. If no one knows a DJ, try the Yellow Pages or check with wedding planners or dance clubs for recommended contacts. The Internet is another useful source, as DJs advertise on Web pages and in MySpace and often link to one another.

Once you find a likely candidate, invite him or her to a planning meeting with your Teen Advisory Board volunteers. Outline the plan you have so far and explain the time frame; also discuss having volunteers to help with setup and cleanup, the payment, appropriate music for the audience, and the policy if a teen brings music. Discuss with the DJ a possible agenda for the workshop series.

Step 4: Create a Program Format and Agenda

Each session begins with a review of the previous lesson, followed by the introduction of a new technique. Everyone gets hands-on experience for the last half hour of the program. The following program agenda shows the timing and order of the one-hour program that was presented at our library:

15 minutes	Review lesson from last session
15 minutes	Introduce new technique
30 minutes	Hands-on activity
End session	

The new techniques portion introduces new terms, explains equipment, and demonstrates what can be done. The hands-on portion gives the teens an opportunity to try out their new knowledge.

"How-To DJ: Skills, Attitudes and Basic Mixing Techniques" at http://bpmdj.yellowcouch.org/djskills.html provides a nice overview of DJ skills if you want to adapt the program so that you can teach it yourself.

Step 5: Market the Program

Word-of-mouth advertising will help promote this program, as teens will talk about it to their friends. Make flyers or rave cards like those shown in Figures 1.1 and 1.2 to distribute to the schools and library branches and for teens to pass out at the various places where they hang out. Contact youth organizations such as the Boys & Girls Clubs, the YMCA, community centers, and homeschooling organizations to further promote the program.

Use colorful graphics in the flyers and posters, and coordinate them visually so they are all recognizable as promoting the same event (as in Figures 1.1 and 1.2). Include any identifying logos or information your library may require. Remember to include Who, What, Where, and When the event will be. Rave cards are postcard-sized flyers that can be printed two or four per page on card stock. They are fun to pass around or mail like postcards.

Step 6: Gather Materials

Collect books and magazines on music and entertainment, CDs from the music collection, and music videos from the DVD collection. Arrange in displays around the program room. Provide handouts, bookmarks, or bibliographies of related materials.

Book List

Broughton, Frank and Bill Brewster. 2003. *How to DJ Right: The Art and Science of Playing Records*. New York: Grove Press.

Hagerman, Andrew. 2005. *Digital Music Making for Teens*. Boston: Thomson Course Technology.

Owsinski, Bobby. 2006. *The Mixing Engineer's Handbook*. Boston: Thomson Course Technology.

Reeves, Diane Lindsey, Karlitz Gai, and Don Rauf. 2005. *Career Ideas for Teens in the Arts and Communications*. New York: Ferguson, an imprint of Facts on Files.

Richards, Chris. 2002. *Teen Spirits Music and Identity in Media Education*. Bristol, PA: UCL Press.

Souvignier, Todd. 2003. The World of DJs and the Turntable Culture. Milwaukee: Hal Leonard Corp.

Steventon, John. 2006. *DJ'ing for Dummies*. Chichester: John Wiley.

Taylor, Chandra Sparks. 2007. *Spin It Like That*. New York: KimaniTRU.

Zemon, Stacy. 2003. *Mobile DJ Handbook: How to Start and Run a Profitable Mobile Disc Jockey Service*. Burlington, MA: Focal Press.

Step 7: Set Up the Program Area

The DJ may want assistance to set up the equipment on the day of the program. Hand trucks or dollies may help with the task. Assign teen volunteers to this job (and to clean

Figure 1.1. DJ Workshop Publicity Flyer

Figure 1.2. DJ Workshop Rave Card

up). They can also set up chairs for the class portion of the program, arranged according to the DJ's preference.

Step 8: Conduct the Event

Take care of any housekeeping announcements first, such as where the restroom is and what the session plan is. Introduce the DJ, and let him or her take over the lesson. Stay in the room to help manage the teens when they are taking turns with the hands-on portion of the class and to take care of any problems.

Step 9: Evaluate the Program

Evaluations are helpful for planning future programs. Customize the evaluation form from Part I (see Figure I.3 on the CD) for participants to fill out. Collect the forms as the audience leaves.

2
HOMEWORK SEMINAR

PROGRAM DESCRIPTION

Students are assigned homework daily, but do they really know how to study and get the most out of their time? The homework seminar is a workshop to show students how to organize and plan their study time. Topics covered include setting study goals, organizing your courses, planning time to study, a winning schedule, finding a place to study, items you should have on hand when studying, and making a study aid and a successful student checklist. Your target audience for this workshop can be students, teachers, parents, or all of the above. Note that this program can be customized for a classroom research project, including instruction on how to do research, what materials are available, and how to do bibliographies for a particular topic.

PROGRAM GOALS

This program is a partnership between the library and the schools to teach students how to organize their study time, supporting educational goals and highlighting the value of the library for teens. This program nurtures in teens a commitment to learning (Developmental Assets® #21–25).

HOW TO DO IT

Step 1: Make a Plan

Solicit volunteers from the library personnel to help staff the classes. If the program is done in the school classroom, teachers can help. The teen librarian can conduct the workshop. Contact the schools, beginning with the administrator's office, and explain the service you are offering. The administrator will encourage the teachers to take advantage of the service and will give you contact information for the teachers. Depending on the distance between the library and the school, the classes may be offered in the school or at the library.

Step 2: Set a Date, Book a Space

The Homework Seminar can be held on a Saturday near the beginning of the school year or during an evening after school. The seminars can be held once a month, once a quarter, or as often as there is sufficient interest. At Fort Worth Public Library, the seminars took place during the school year.

The Teen Center of the Central Library was an ideal location for our class. You need a space for tables and chairs for the students and a projector and screen. This seminar can also be taken on the road to locations outside the library, such as schools, community centers, and Boys & Girls Clubs. If there is sufficient interest, seminars might be held in various library branches.

Step 3: Book the Presenter

The library's teen specialist or a staff member of the teen department familiar with working with students can design and organize the lesson. A college student with good research skills would also be a good candidate.

Step 4: Create a Program Format and Agenda

The following is a sample Homework Seminar agenda for a one-hour session:

- Welcome, announcements, and introductions
- PowerPoint presentation
- Questions and answers
- End of session

Step 5: Market the Program

In order to teach one, you must first reach one. To reach teens you must go where they are to get them to come to you. Tell your local homeschool association about the program. Go to the school and Parent Teacher Association meetings to promote the program. Let parents know that you offer free additional assistance to help their young person succeed in school. Let teachers know of your resources and that you are there to help them. Contacting local youth organizations can also help you to reach teens. Many of these organizations are looking for programs that they can either take their members to or host in their facility. Many, like the Boys & Girls Clubs and the YMCA or the YWCA, have their own transportation. Create and distribute flyers like the example in Figure 2.1. Teen Advisory Board members can help promote the program by distributing the flyers.

Step 6: Gather Materials, Prepare Handouts

You will need a laptop with the PowerPoint program, a video projector and screen, and the necessary cables and extension cords. Some libraries and classrooms will have a room set up with the necessary equipment, and others will need you to bring it. A flip chart might be helpful. Create handouts listing the homework resources your library offers, such as homework links and tutoring programs. Bring handouts, bookmarks, paper, and pencils for the students. Prepare the PowerPoint presentation for the program by adapting the Homework Seminar PowerPoint program on the accompanying CD (and shown in Figure 2.2). Gather books and other materials that discuss school life and study skills for displays.

Book List

Cerra, Cheli and Ruth Jacoby. 2006. *Homework Talk! : The Art of Effective Communication About Your Child's Homework*. San Francisco: Jossey-Bass.

Conley, David T. 2005. *College Knowledge: What It Really Takes for Students to Succeed and What We Can Do to Get Them Ready*. San Francisco: Jossey-Bass.

Dyson, Marianne J. 2000. *Homework Help on the Internet*. New York: Scholastic Reference.

Figure 2.1. Homework Seminar Publicity Flyer

Don't agonize over your homework

Get Help!

From the

Homework Seminar

\<DATE, TIME, AND LOCATION\>

Parents Welcome!

Topics:

Setting Study Goals

Organizing Your Courses

Planning Time to Study

Successful Student Checklist

Sponsored by \<LIBRARY NAME\>

\<LIBRARY LOGO\>

To make arrangements for sign-language interpretation, call
\<PHONE/TDD NUMBERS\> at least 48 hours in advance.

Figure 2.2. Homework Seminar PowerPoint Presentation

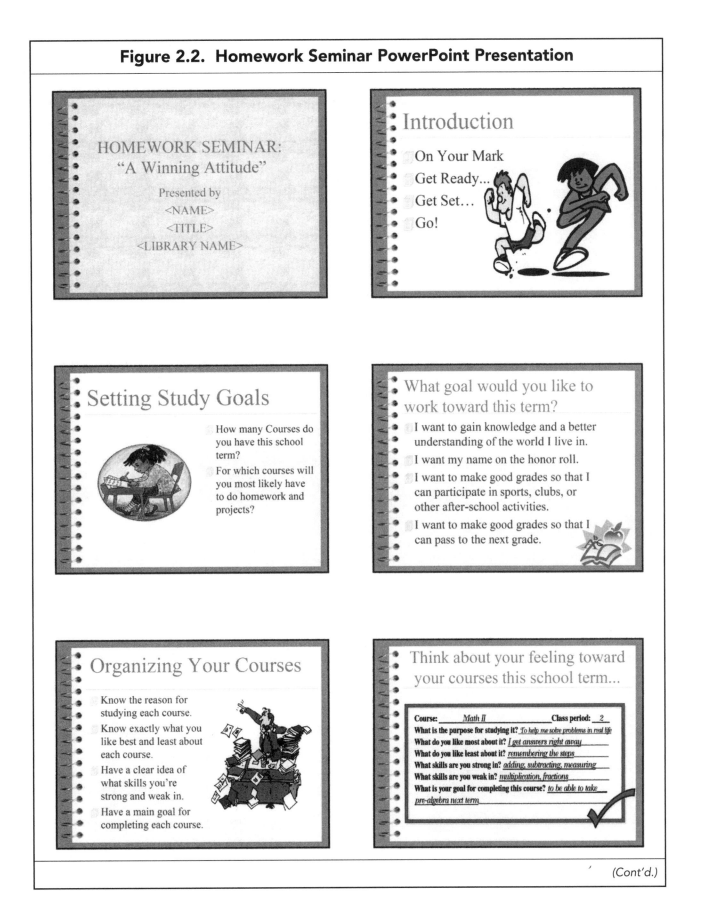

(Cont'd.)

Figure 2.2. Homework Seminar PowerPoint Presentation *(Continued)*

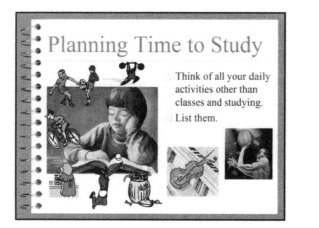

Planning Time to Study

Think of all your daily activities other than classes and studying.
List them.

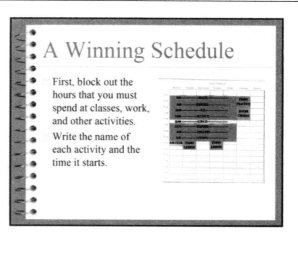

A Winning Schedule

First, block out the hours that you must spend at classes, work, and other activities.

Write the name of each activity and the time it starts.

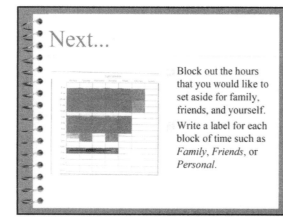

Next...

Block out the hours that you would like to set aside for family, friends, and yourself.

Write a label for each block of time such as *Family*, *Friends*, or *Personal*.

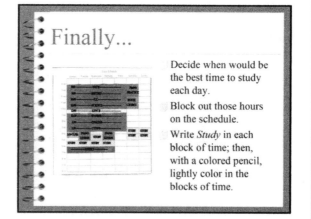

Finally...

Decide when would be the best time to study each day.

Block out those hours on the schedule.

Write *Study* in each block of time; then, with a colored pencil, lightly color in the blocks of time.

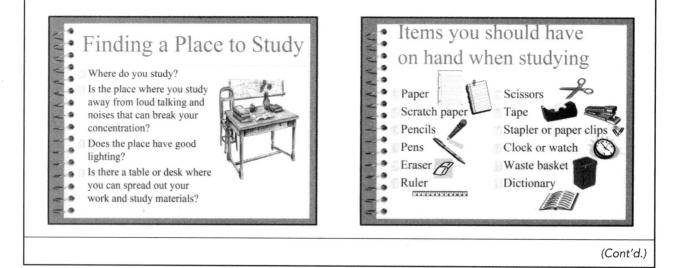

Finding a Place to Study

Where do you study?

Is the place where you study away from loud talking and noises that can break your concentration?

Does the place have good lighting?

Is there a table or desk where you can spread out your work and study materials?

Items you should have on hand when studying

Paper
Scratch paper
Pencils
Pens
Eraser
Ruler

Scissors
Tape
Stapler or paper clips
Clock or watch
Waste basket
Dictionary

(Cont'd.)

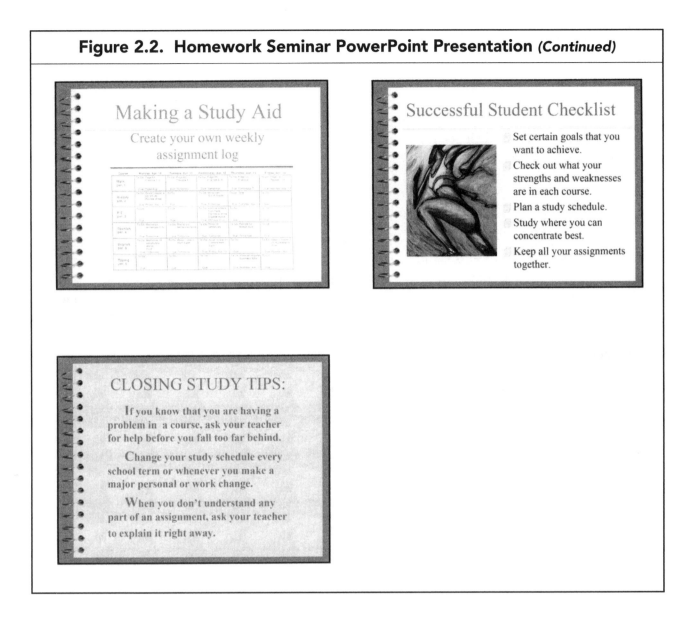

Figure 2.2. Homework Seminar PowerPoint Presentation *(Continued)*

James, Elizabeth and Carol Barkin. 1998. *How to Be School Smart: Super Study Skills*. Brookfield, CT: Millbrook Press.

Keizer, Gregg. 1996. *The FamilyPC Guide to Homework*. New York: Hyperion.

Lockett, Sharon Marshall. 2007. *Home, Sweet Homework: A Parent's Guide to Stress-Free Homework & Studying Strategies That Work*. Avon, MA: Adams Media.

McEwan, Elaine K. 1996. *The Dog Ate It: Conquering Homework Hassles*. Wheaton, IL: Harold Shaw Publishers.

Mediavilla, Cindy. 2001. *Creating the Full-Service Homework Center in Your Library*. Chicago: American Library Association.

Nathan, Amy and Anne Canevari Green. 1996. *Surviving Homework: Tips from Teens*. New York: Lothrop, Lee & Shepard Books.

Schumm, Jeanne Shay. 2005. *How to Help Your Child with Homework: The Complete Guide to Encouraging Good Study Habits and Ending the Homework Wars*. Minneapolis: Free Spirit.

Stein, Judith. 2007. *Parent Guide to Hassle-free Homework*. New York: Scholastic.
Trumbauer, Lisa. 2000. *Cool Sites: Homework Help for Kids on the Net*. Brookfield, CT: Millbrook Press.

Step 7: Set Up the Program Area

Set up tables and chairs, laptop, and projector so that all the audience members can see the screen. Distribute paper, pencils, and handouts. Set up displays you have created of the books about school life and studying.

Step 8: Conduct the Event

Introduce yourself and any library staff with you. If you are working with a partner, you might share the presentation. Two presenters can be more interesting if they work well together. Present the PowerPoint, allowing students to ask questions as you go along. Tell students about any homework assistance programs, homework help links, and tutoring programs your library may offer. Some students may have specific questions about an assignment, so decide if you will refer them to the reference department or try to answer the questions during the program.

Step 9: Evaluate the Program

Evaluations are helpful for planning future programs. Customize the evaluation form from Part I (see Figure I.3 on the CD) for participants to fill out. Collect the forms as the audience leaves.

3
MINDING YOUR OWN BUSINESS SEMINAR

PROGRAM DESCRIPTION

The one-day Minding Your Own Business Seminar provides information and resources for people who want to start a small business. Along with the business instruction, teens will learn to make jewelry in a Beading Workshop as an example of a small business they can easily run. Jewelry making can be a relatively inexpensive enterprise as a workshop and also as a start-up business.

PROGRAM GOALS

The seminar is an opportunity to expose teens to books on entrepreneurship as a career and to books on beading. Increase library sign-ups by requiring a library card for attendance to the seminar. The program helps teens to make constructive use of their time (Developmental Assets® #17–20) and nurtures, celebrates, and affirms a positive identity (Developmental Assets #37–40).

HOW TO DO IT

Step 1: Make a Plan

The planning meeting should include the community relations representative of a potential funding organization. Our program was sponsored by Wal-Mart, but a community club or another business like Target may be a good resource. It is best to have all program details finalized before you meet with organization representatives when you are seeking funds. They will need information such as the name of your project or program, who will it benefit and how, and, of course, how much will it cost. Teens always appreciate refreshments, so include this expense in your plans.

The accompanying hands-on workshop does not have to be on making jewelry. You can choose another venture to give participants an example of how they can go into business for themselves. Limit your class size to fit your budget for materials and refreshments.

Step 2: Set a Date, Book a Space

The Minding Your Own Business Seminar can be held on one day or as a series of different programs on separate days. Our seminar was a one-day event held on the Saturday before Mother's Day. Schedule one to one and a half hours for each program in the seminar.

The seminar can take place in a library meeting room or in the teen area if it is large enough, or it can be taken on the road to other locations. You will need a space with tables and chairs for the teens.

Step 3: Book the Presenter

The leader for the business part of the seminar can be a library staff member who is familiar with small business start-up or a library patron or community member who has successfully started a small business. You will also need someone to lead the Beading Workshop. A staff member, a patron who is crafty, and a bead craft shop owner are good candidates, or you might learn to do it yourself from a library book!

Step 4: Create a Program Format and Agenda

- Make an opening statement about the purpose of the seminar.
- Present information on entrepreneurship.
- Introduce the beading instructor.
- Conduct the Beading Workshop as a hands-on activity.
- Pass out handouts on basic beading information and an entrepreneurship book list.
- Answer any questions participants may have at this time.
- End the seminar with closing words on teens going into business for themselves as a way to help finance their college education.

Step 5: Market the Program

Produce flyers (as in Figure 3.1), posters, and rave cards to advertise the events, and distribute them to the schools, Boys & Girls Clubs, community centers, and homeschooling organizations. Ask the Teen Advisory Board to distribute rave cards where teens hang out. Distribute flyers and rave cards to other library branches. Post flyers at recreation centers such as the YMCA.

Step 6: Gather Materials, Prepare the Handouts

Gather books, magazines, and instructional DVDs about beading and entrepreneurship to display in the program room. Create a handout for the Beading Workshop. It should contain the information shown in Figure 3.2, which was created by Alice Howell, the certified beading instructor who led our workshop.

Prepare beading materials in individual packet sets. The beading project can vary according to your budget and availability of supplies. Suggested easy-to-make projects are anklets, bracelets, and necklaces. Select beads that boys and girls will like if you want to attract both audiences. In each package you will need the flexible wire or beading thread, the beads for the project, and a clasp for the ends.

Book List

Abrams, Rhonda M. and Julie Vallone. 2005. *Business Plan in a Day: Get It Done Right, Get It Done Fast*. Palo Alto, CA: The Planning Shop.

Baker, Diane and Alexandra Michaels, illus. 2001. *Jazzy Jewelry: Power Beads, Crystals, Chokers, & Illusion and Tattoo Styles*. Charlotte, VT: Williamson Pub.

Bhatt, Sonal. 2002. *Totally Beads*. New York: Sterling.

Blanchard, Kenneth H., Don Hutson, and Ethan Willis. 2008. *The One Minute Entrepreneur: The Secret to Creating and Sustaining a Successful Business*. New York: Currency Doubleday.

Figure 3.1. Minding Your Own Business Seminar Publicity Flyer

Join the Teen Advisory Board
in the
<TEEN CENTER>

Sign up for

"Minding Your
Own Business"
**An Entrepreneurial
Seminar for Teens**

Learn how to

Make Jewelry
in
Beading Basics
a Hands-On Workshop

<DATE AND TIME>

Reserve your place NOW at <LOCATION>.

Seating Is Limited!

<LIBRARY
LOGO>

To make arrangements for sign-language interpretation, call
<PHONE/TDD NUMBERS> at least 48 hours in advance.

Figure 3.2. Beading Basics Handout for the Beading Workshop

Beading Basics

Tools

The tools needed for making beaded jewelry are fairly basic and inexpensive. Jewelry makers' pliers and wire cutters are essential tools, along with beading needles, knotting tweezers, scissors, bead boards, and glue.

> *Round-nose pliers*
> *Chain-nose/long-nose pliers*
> *Crimping pliers*
> *Split-ring pliers*
> *Diagonal pliers*
> *Bent-nose pliers*

Flexible Beading Wire

Flexible beading wire is composed of wires twisted together and coated with nylon. This wire is stronger than thread and does not stretch. The higher the strand count, the more flexible and kink-resistant the wire is.

Memory Wire

Memory wire is a stiff, pre-coiled wire that will return to its original shape after being pulled apart.

Monofilament Nylon Beading Thread or Nymo

Monofilament thread is an omni-flex wire that is clear and pound (lb) tested for strength.

Findings

Findings are used to put beads, thread, and/or wire together to make jewelry. Findings include, but are not limited to, clasps, jump rings, split-rings, crimp beads, bails, bead caps, spacer beads/bars, fishhook clasps, barrel clasps, toggle clasps, or bar and ring clasps.

Flattened Crimp: Basic Technique

Hold the crimp bead using the tip of your chain-nose/long-nose pliers. Squeeze the pliers firmly to flatten the crimp. Tug the clasp to make sure the crimp has a solid grip on the wire. If it slides, remove the crimp bead and repeat the steps with the new crimp bead.

Source: Courtesy of Alice Howell, certified beading instructor.

Bolles, Richard Nelson, Carol Christen, and Jean M. Blomquist. 2006. *What Color Is Your Parachute? For Teens: Discovering Yourself, Defining Your Future*. Berkeley, CA: Ten Speed Press.

Chambers, K. Dennis. 2008. *The Entrepreneur's Guide to Writing Business Plans and Proposals*. Westport, CT: Praeger.

Clark, Maxine K. and Amy Joyner. 2006. *The Bear Necessities of Business: Building a Company with Heart*. New York: Wiley.

Covello, Joseph A. and Brian J. Hazelgren. 2005. *Your First Business Plan: A Simple Question-and-Answer Format Designed to Help You Write Your Own Plan*. Naperville, IL: Sourcebooks.

Fujimoto, Naomi. 2007. *Cool Jewels: Beading Projects for Teens*. Waukesha, WI: Kalmbach Publishing.

Harper, Stephen C. 1991. *The McGraw-Hill Guide to Starting Your Own Business: A Step-by-Step Blueprint for the First-Time Entrepreneur*. New York: McGraw-Hill.

Harrington, Judith B. and Richard Mintzer. 2006. *The Everything Start Your Own Business Book: From Financing to Making Your First Sale, All You Need to Get Your Business Off the Ground*. Avon, MA: Adams Media.

Powell, Michelle. 2002. *Beadwork*. Chicago: Heinemann Library.

Sadler, Judy Ann and June Bradford, illus. 2005. Hemp Jewelry. Tonawanda, NY: Kids Can Press.

Scheunemann, Pam. 2005. *Cool Beaded Jewelry*. Edina, MN: Abdo.

Solovic, Susan Wilson. 2008. *The Girls' Guide to Building a Million-Dollar Business*. New York: AMACOM Books.

Speechley, Greta. 2003. *Bead Book*. Danbury, CT: Grolier Incorporated.

Stull, Katherine. 2006. *20-Minute Crafts: Beading: Hands-on Crafts for Kids*. New York: Sterling.

Step 7: Set Up the Program Area

Set up tables and chairs. Distribute jewelry packets and any tools the participants might need (scissors, wire cutters, crimpers, etc.) to each table. A Styrofoam tray or plate for each teen can help keep the beading supplies separated and on the tables. Set up the book displays on entrepreneurship and beading, and distribute the handouts.

Step 8: Conduct the Event

Follow the agenda. Deliver the lecture, leaving time for questions and discussion. Then conduct the Beading Workshop.

Step 9: Evaluate the Program

Evaluations are helpful for planning future programs. Customize the evaluation form from Part I (see Figure I.3 on the CD) for participants to fill out. Collect the forms as the audience leaves.

4
POETRY WORKSHOP

PROGRAM DESCRIPTION

The Poetry Workshop series helps teens learn to express their feelings in poetry. Held once a month, the series ends in a Poetry Slam, which is a poetry competition. Local poets and/or teachers facilitate the workshops.

PROGRAM GOALS

The Poetry Workshops are designed to educate youth and help them develop a positive attitude toward poetry. The workshops encourage teenagers to come to the library and learn about the poetry collection. The teens will view the library as a "cool" place to be. This program helps establish clear boundaries and foster high expectations (Developmental Assets® #11–16), helps teens find activities that make constructive use of their time (Developmental Assets #17–20), nurtures in teens a commitment to learning (Developmental Assets #21–25), instills positive values to guide them (Developmental Assets #26–31), helps teens develop life skills and social competencies (Developmental Assets #32–36), and nurtures, celebrates, and affirms their positive identity (Developmental Assets #37–40).

HOW TO DO IT

Step 1: Make a Plan

Recruit a local poet, poetry group, or English teacher to lead the workshops. Schedule a planning meeting with the workshop leader(s) and the Teen Advisory Board to discuss the content and length of the workshops and decide on an agenda. Consider serving refreshments. At the Fort Worth Public Library we had chips and drinks. You can also conduct a poetry workshop yourself. Topics for sessions you might consider are Creative Writing: From Visual to Verbal, How to Create Original Works of Poetry, How to Combine Music and the Spoken Word in Poetry, and Different Types of Poetry: Ode, Song, Haiku, Free Verse, Sonnet, Tongue Twisters.

Step 2: Set a Date, Book a Space

Our monthly workshops took place every fourth Saturday for six months. A similar schedule may work for you. The group may be interested in continuing the workshops after the series is over! The workshops can take place in the teen area if there is adequate space or in a meeting room.

Step 3: Book the Presenter

An English teacher, a local poet, or members of a local poetry group are good candidates for leading this workshop. The presenter may charge a fee; if so, discuss how many workshop sessions you can afford in your budget. If you need additional funds, contact a civic club or a local business that supports community activities. Be prepared to explain exactly what you want to do, how much it would cost, and who your audience will be.

Step 4: Create a Program Format and Agenda

The poetry group can plan the workshop formats. Activities might include playing music and writing about how the music makes you feel or writing exercises experimenting with different forms of poetry, such as haiku, sonnets, or cinquains. Haiku is a Japanese form of poetry composed of three lines of five, seven, and five syllables, respectively. A sonnet is 14 lines written in iambic pentameter (ten syllables per line) with a specific rhyming pattern: a-b-a-b / c-d-c-d / e-f-e-f / g-g. A cinquain is a five-line poem that describes a person, place, or thing. Program 14, "Poetry Slam" describes how to conduct the final session.

Step 5: Market the Program

Create flyers, posters, and rave cards to advertise the events and distribute to schools, Boys & Girls Clubs, homeschoolers' organizations, local youth organizations, and teen hot spots and centers. Figure 4.1 shows a sample publicity flyer.

Step 6: Gather Materials

You will need pencils and paper for each teen. Poetry journals and pens are nice to give to the teens if your budget allows. If you can buy only one or two, use them for door prizes. Assemble poetry and writing books as a display.

Book List

Alderson, Daniel. 1996. *Talking Back to Poems: A Working Guide for the Aspiring Poet.* Berkeley, CA: Celestial Arts.

Burkhardt, Ross M. 2006. *Using Poetry in the Classroom: Engaging Students in Learning.* Lanham, MD: Rowman & Littlefield Education.

Day, Lucille and Doug Dworkin. 2005. *Chain Letter.* Berkeley, CA: Heyday Books.

Fletcher, Ralph J. 2002. *Poetry Matters: Writing a Poem from the Inside Out.* New York: HarperTrophy.

Hewitt, Geof. 1998. *Today You Are My Favorite Poet: Writing Poems with Teenagers.* Portsmouth, NH: Heinemann.

Livingston, Myra Cohn. 1991. *Poem-making: Ways to Begin Writing Poetry.* New York: HarperCollins Publishers.

Mock, Jeff. 1998. *You Can Write Poetry.* Cincinnati: Writer's Digest Books.

Weiss, Jen and Scott Herndon. 2001. *Brave New Voices: The Youth Speaks Guide to Teaching Spoken-word Poetry.* Portsmouth, NH: Heinemann.

Wong, Janet S. and Theresa Flavin, illus. 2002. *You Have to Write.* New York: Margaret K. McElderry Books.

Step 7: Set Up the Program Area

You need tables and chairs for the teens and a table for light refreshments, if served.

Figure 4.1. Poetry Workshop Publicity Flyer

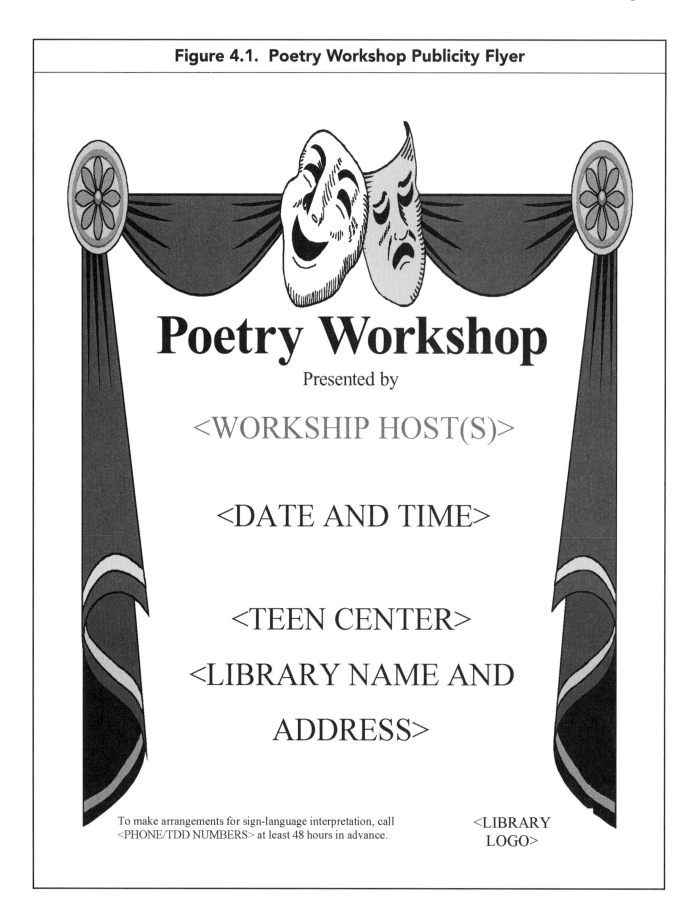

Poetry Workshop

Presented by

\<WORKSHIP HOST(S)\>

\<DATE AND TIME\>

\<TEEN CENTER\>

\<LIBRARY NAME AND

ADDRESS\>

To make arrangements for sign-language interpretation, call
\<PHONE/TDD NUMBERS\> at least 48 hours in advance.

\<LIBRARY
LOGO\>

Step 8: Conduct the Event

Introduce yourself and make any housekeeping announcements (where the restrooms are, etc.). Introduce the poetry group leaders and let them conduct the workshop. Stay in the room to help keep order.

Step 9: Evaluate the Program

Evaluations are helpful for planning future programs. Customize the evaluation form from Part I (see Figure I.3 on CD) for participants to fill out. Collect the forms as the audience leaves.

5
TEEN TALENT INCUBATOR

PROGRAM DESCRIPTION

The Teen Talent Incubator is a biweekly series of workshops instructed by entertainment industry professionals to teach young musicians how to improve their talents.

PROGRAM GOALS

The workshop helps talented teens kick-start their careers and spotlights specific library collections. Teen Talent Incubator is a learning experience for the entire family, teaching young people the business side of the music industry. The program supports teens with love, care, and attention (Developmental Assets® #1–6), empowers them with opportunities to make a difference in their family and community (Developmental Assets #7–10), establishes clear boundaries and high expectations (Developmental Assets #11–16), nurtures a commitment to learning (Developmental Assets #21–25), helps teens develop life skills and social competencies (Developmental Assets #32–36), and nurtures, celebrates, and affirms a positive identity (Developmental Assets #37–40).

HOW TO DO IT

Step 1: Make a Plan

Ask music industry professionals to volunteer to facilitate the workshops. Volunteers from the library personnel will staff the workshops. There is no cost to the participants. Possible topics to include in the workshop are the music industry, music production, songwriting, music as an occupation, copyright, and helpful tips in the industry.

Step 2: Set a Date, Book a Space

Schedule the workshops biweekly for one hour per session. The proposed dates are every first and third Thursday. Schedule the industry professionals who will participate. A large room is needed and, ideally, additional rooms for breakout sessions.

Step 3: Book the Presenter

Arrange meetings with music industry professionals such as an entertainment attorney, a representative from a record label, a recording studio owner, a music artist, a producer, and a songwriter. Discuss the purpose of the series and ask them to participate by leading one of the sessions. Have them fill out an information sheet (Figure 5.1) to help you organize the program agenda. This program is intended to help teens improve on talents they already have, so including trainers in voice or instrument to give valuable tips to individual teens would be ideal.

Figure 5.1. Teen Talent Incubator Workshop Presenter Information Sheet

Teen Talent Incubator
Workshop Presenter Information Sheet

Name of Company or Organization _____

Representative's Name _____

Position and/or Title _____

Address _____

City _____ State _____ Zip _____

Phone _____ E-mail_____

Preferred contact method _____

Brief Bio (attach additional sheet if necessary):

_____

_____

_____

_____

_____

_____

_____

_____

_____

_____

_____

_____

_____

_____

_____

_____

_____

Step 4: Create a Program Format and Agenda

15 minutes	Review lesson from last meeting
30 minutes	Introduce guest speakers, who conduct informal discussion with question and answer session
30 minutes	Conduct hands-on exercise and breakout session, working on individual talents
15 minutes	Assign homework
End session	

Step 5: Market the Program

Produce flyers and rave cards (see examples in Figures 5.2 and 5.3) to advertise the event and distribute them to the schools, Boys & Girls Clubs, community centers, and the YWCA. Ask Teen Advisory Board members to distribute rave cards to teen hangouts.

Step 6: Gather Materials, Prepare Handouts

Prepare a participant information sheet (see Figure 5.4). Have all participants fill one out before the programs begin. This will help you recruit professionals of interest to the teens. The form will also allow you to use photos of the music session in your publicity. Have teens sign in for each session (see sign-up sheet in Figure 5.5). Assemble and display books of interest during the programs.

Book List

Belleville, Nyree. 2000. *Booking, Promoting and Marketing Your Music: A Complete Guide for Bands and Solo Artists*. Vallejo, CA: MixBooks.

Bloom, Benjamin Samuel and Lauren A. Sosniak. 1985. *Developing Talent in Young People*. New York: Ballantine Books.

Borg, Bobby. 2008. *The Musician's Handbook: A Practical Guide to Understanding the Music Business*. New York: Billboard Books/Watson-Guptill Publications.

Borwick, John. 1980. *Sound Recording Practice: A Handbook. Association of Professional Recording Studios*. New York: Oxford University Press,

Cefrey, Holly. 2003. *Backstage at a Music Video*. New York: Children's Press.

Dean, Peter. 2002. *Production Management: Making Shows Happen*. Wiltshire, England: Crowood Press.

Hall, Eleanor G. and Nancy Skinner. 1980. *Somewhere to Turn: Strategies for Parents of Gifted and Talented Children*. New York: Teachers College, Columbia University.

Haring, Bruce. 2005. *How Not to Destroy Your Career in Music: Avoiding the Common Mistakes Most Musicians Make*. Los Angeles: Lone Eagle.

Heylin, Clinton. 1995. *Bootleg: The Secret History of the Other Recording Industry*. New York: St. Martin's Press.

Honnold, RoseMary. 2005. *More Teen Programs That Work*. New York: Neal-Schuman.

Koller, Fred. 2001. *How to Pitch and Promote Your Songs*. New York: Allworth Press.

Maxwell, John C. 2007. *Talent Is Never Enough: Discover the Choices That Will Take You Beyond Your Talent*. Nashville: Thomas Nelson.

Nathan, Amy. 2000. *The Young Musician's Survival Guide: Tips from Teens & Pros*. New York: Oxford University Press.

Figure 5.2. Teen Talent Incubator Workshop Publicity Flyer

Teen Talent Incubator

Bi-weekly workshops instructed by Entertainment Industry professionals

Improve Your Talent

Kick-Start Your Music Career

<TEEN CENTER>

<LIBRARY NAME AND ADDRESS>

<DATE AND TIME>

<LIBRARY LOGO>

To make arrangements for sign-language interpretation, call <PHONE/TDD NUMBERS> at least 48 hours in advance.

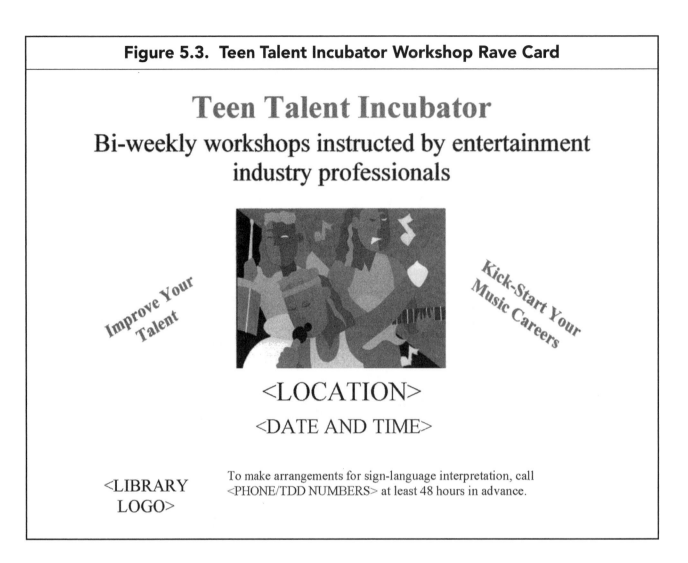

Figure 5.3. Teen Talent Incubator Workshop Rave Card

Pickow, Peter and Amy Appleby. 1988. *The Billboard Book of Songwriting*. New York: Billboard Publications.

Schwartz, Daylle Deanna. 2005. *I Don't Need a Record Deal! Your Survival Guide for the Indie Music Revolution*. New York: Billboard.

Simmons, Russell and Rebecca Chaiklin. 2006. *Russell Simmons' Hip-Hop Laws of Success*. Chatsworth, CA: Simmons-Lathan Media Group: Image Entertainment.

Stone, Cliffie and Joan Carol Stone. 2000. *You Gotta Be Bad Before You Can Be Good! Talent Shows & Beyond*. Hollywood, CA: Showdown.

Thall, Peter M. 2006. *What They'll Never Tell You About the Music Business: The Myths, the Secrets, the Lies (& a Few Truths)*. New York: Billboard.

Weissman, Dick. 1997. *The Music Business: Career Opportunities and Self-defense*. New York: Three Rivers Press.

Step 7: Set Up Program Area

Set up chairs around a stage area. Set up sound equipment. Set up participant check-in table with sign-in sheet. Create book and other material displays, and place them around the room.

Figure 5.4. Teen Talent Incubator Workshop Participant Information and Release Form

Teen Talent Incubator Workshop
Participant Information and Release Form

Name of participant _____

Age of participant_____

Contact person _____

Address _____

City _____ State _____ Zip _____

Phone _____ E-mail _____

Preferred contact method_____

Type of talent_____

Brief bio of individual (attach additional sheet if necessary):

_____

_____

_____

_____

_____

Minor participants must have their parent's or guardian's permission. Each participant must have a release form on file.

Permission / Release Form:

Permission is hereby granted for the library to use my name, likeness, and photograph, or the name, likeness, and photograph of a minor child, regarding the Teen Talent Incubator for editorial, public relations, promotional, and advertising purposes on behalf of the Fort Worth Public Library. Permission is also hereby granted for the use of my image and/or voice, or the image and/or voice of a minor child, to be video-taped and cable cast regarding this event.

Permission is hereby granted by:

Parent or Guardian Signature: _____

Printed Name: _____

Participant's Name:_____

Participant's Printed Name: _____

Date: _____

This release must be received prior to performing.

Figure 5.5. Teen Talent Incubator Workshop Participant Sign-In Sheet

Teen Talent Incubator Workshop
Participant Sign-In Sheet

Date: _____

Name	Age	Phone #	E-Mail Address

Step 8: Conduct the Event

At the workshops we displayed the books and discussed the library's collection of information on the music industry. Each session had a guest speaker. The classes included discussions with industry professionals and an opportunity for participants to work with the professionals one on one, asking questions and practicing their skills. For example, if the professional was a drummer, he would work with the drummers and give them tips on how to improve their skills and so on. Each workshop ended with a general homework assignment to be completed outside of class.

Step 9: Evaluate the Program

Evaluations are helpful for planning future programs. Customize the evaluation form from Part I (see Figure I.3 on CD) for participants to fill out. Collect the forms as the audience leaves.

6
TEEN TOP MODELS FASHION COURSE

PROGRAM DESCRIPTION

America's Next Top Model is a very popular television production. Many teen girls and teen guys aspire to become top models. To be successful in the modeling and fashion industries, teens need to become familiar with the necessary competencies in employability, communication, and visual presentation. Fashion industry professionals help teach this modeling course for teens between the ages of 13 and 19 over a four-week period. Each participant will receive a Certificate of Completion from the library along with a five-photo portfolio (optional, depending on funding) to be presented at the End-of-the-Course Fashion Show.

PROGRAM GOALS

Families and friends can support their teens in this opportunity. Hosting a fashion modeling course at the library will promote and increase teen usage and awareness of the library. Each participant must own a library card, which increases library card sign-ups. Those who do not have a card must fill out an application upon registration. Teens must be able to commit two hours a day, one day a week, for four consecutive weeks. Upon completion of the modeling course, teens should be able to:

- Create auditory and visual presentations
- Design a model's photograph and fashion portfolio
- Illustrate writing skills by preparing a personal résumé
- Select a variety of visual poses and types of runway walking
- Apply professional ethics and etiquette skills
- Participate in composing and choreographing a fashion show

This program empowers teens with opportunities to make a difference in their family and community (Developmental Assets® #7–10), establishes clear boundaries and has high expectations (Developmental Assets #11–16), helps teens find activities that make constructive use of their time (Developmental Assets #17–20), nurtures in them a commitment to learning (Developmental Assets #21–25), and nurtures, celebrates, and affirms their positive identity (Developmental Assets #37–40).

HOW TO DO IT

Step 1: Make a Plan

Post a notice for teens between 13 and 19 years of age in the library. Teens must be able to commit two hours a day, one day a week, for four consecutive weeks. Fashion industry professionals will help teach the four-week course.

Each participant will receive a Certificate of Completion along with a five-photo portfolio (if included as part of the program) to be presented at the End-of-the-Course Fashion Show to be held in the meeting room on the day of the final class. Invite parents, relatives, and friends to attend the closing ceremony.

Notify and invite the news media to attend the final event. Serve refreshments (such as cookies and soft drinks) after the closing ceremony. The cost to produce the program will vary depending on the cost of the photographer for the portfolios (if included in the program).

Step 2: Set a Date, Book a Space

Our Teen Top Models Fashion Course was held on four Wednesdays in June from 6 to 8 p.m. The closing ceremony was held the following week, also on Wednesday.

A meeting room or lecture hall is a suitable setting for the course. Room to accommodate the audience of parents and friends is needed for the closing ceremony.

Step 3: Book the Presenters

Book a beauty consultant (e.g., a Mary Kay consultant) to teach makeup and a beautician to conduct a workshop on hair design. A home economics teacher can do a seminar on etiquette along with a runway coach to teach the models how to walk a runway. For possible partners, contact beauty schools and colleges, high schools, charm schools, and modeling schools. Each presenter will conduct a session. A competent library staff photographer can take the photos, or a local photographer may offer a reduced fee for a library program.

Step 4: Create a Program Format and Agenda

Each session will focus on one aspect of modeling. Meet with each of the presenters to decide what will happen at each session, what supplies and room setup are required, and what assistance will be needed.

Step 5: Market the Program

Produce flyers and rave cards (see examples in Figures 6.1 and 6.2) to advertise the event, and distribute them to the schools, Boys & Girls Clubs, community centers, the YWCA, and so forth. To determine interest and to establish a class count for the presenters, participants must apply in advance. Place program applications/registration forms (see Figure 6.3) around the library and possibly on the library's Web site. Teens should bring a change of outfits for the photos (if portfolios are being offered): business attire, casual, and sports. The photographer should take a head shot, too.

Step 6: Gather Materials, Prepare Handouts

Collect books and magazines about the fashion industry, modeling, makeup, and hairstyles for displays in the program room. Collect materials each presenter may need for each session. Select music or ask your teens for music choices. Prepare a sign-in sheet for each session (see Figure 6.4).

Figure 6.1. Teen Top Models Fashion Course Publicity Flyer

Figure 6.2. Teen Top Models Fashion Course Rave Card

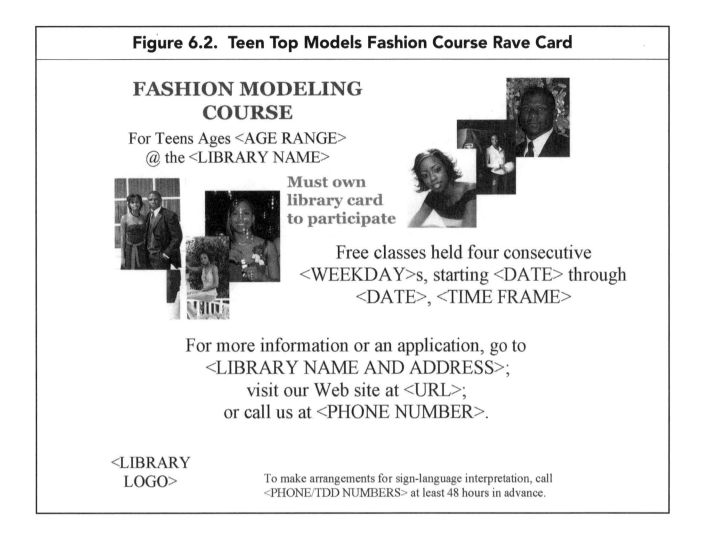

FASHION MODELING COURSE

For Teens Ages <AGE RANGE>
@ the <LIBRARY NAME>

Must own library card to participate

Free classes held four consecutive
<WEEKDAY>s, starting <DATE> through
<DATE>, <TIME FRAME>

For more information or an application, go to
<LIBRARY NAME AND ADDRESS>;
visit our Web site at <URL>;
or call us at <PHONE NUMBER>.

<LIBRARY LOGO>

To make arrangements for sign-language interpretation, call
<PHONE/TDD NUMBERS> at least 48 hours in advance.

Book List

Adams-Geller, Paige, Ashley Borden, and Zibby Right. 2008. *Your Perfect Fit: What to Wear to Show Off Your Assets, What to Do to Tone Up Your Trouble Spots*. New York: McGraw-Hill.

Cox, Susan Linnet. 2006. *Photo Styling: How to Build Your Career and Succeed*. New York: Allworth Press.

Favilla, Emmy. 2008. *Seventeen Presents 500 Style Tips: What to Wear for School, Weekend, Parties & More!* New York: Hearst Books.

Garcia, Nina and Ruben Toledo. 2007. *The Little Black Book of Style*. New York: Harper-Collins.

Gunn, Tim and Kate Moloney. 2007. *A Guide to Quality, Taste, & Style*. New York: Abrams Image.

Hayden. 2008. *A Matter of Attitude*. New York: Kimani TRU Press.

J.G. Ferguson Publishing Company. 2007. *What Can I Do Now? Fashion*. New York: Ferguson.

Jones, Jen. 2007. *Fashion Careers: Finding the Right Fit*. Mankato, MN: Capstone Press.

Jones, Jen. 2007. *Fashion Trends: How Popular Style Is Shaped*. Mankato, MN: Capstone Press.

Figure 6.3. Teen Top Models Fashion Course Participant Information and Registration Form

Teen Top Models Fashion Course
Participant Information and Registration Form

(Please Print Clearly)

COURSE TITLE:	AGE LEVEL:
LOCATION:	COURSE LENGTH:

Major Concepts/Content:

The modeling course is designed to provide teens an opportunity to become familiar with the competencies in employability, communication, and visual presentation required in order to succeed in the modeling and fashion industries.

Major Instructional Activities:

Instructional activities are provided in both classroom and hands-on practical experiences as well as written and creative projects related to course content. Active participation is continually stressed through class discussions, group work, and project compositions. Students investigate various modeling and fashion occupations and participate in a runway fashion show.

Major Evaluative Techniques:

Teens are expected to participate in both written and practical activities. Certificates are awarded to teens based on class participation, completion of course, and the ability to work both independently and cooperatively.

Essential Objectives:

Upon completion of the modeling course, teens should be able to:

- ❑ Create auditory and visual presentations
- ❑ Design a model's photograph and fashion portfolio
- ❑ Illustrate writing skills by preparing a personal résumé
- ❑ Select a variety of visual poses and types of runway walking
- ❑ Apply professional ethics and etiquette skills.
- ❑ Participate in composing and choreographing a fashion show

Registration Requirements:

Teen must possess a library card and be able to commit two hours a day, one day a week, for four consecutive weeks, <INSERT DATES AND TIMES>.

*A signed permission/release form must be submitted prior to the event
(see following page).*

(Cont'd.)

Figure 6.3. Teen Top Models Fashion Course Participant Information and Registration Form *(Continued)*

Teen Top Models Registration Form

Name: _____ Age: _____ Date of Birth: _____

Address: _____ Telephone Number: _____

School: _____ Grade: _____

E-mail Address: _____

Parent's Signature: _____

Permission / Release Form:

Permission is hereby granted for the library to use my name, likeness, and photograph or the name, likeness, and photograph of a minor child, regarding Teen Top Models for editorial, public relations, promotional, and advertising purposes on behalf of the <LIBRARY NAME>.

Permission is also hereby granted for the use of my image and/or voice, or the image and/or voice of a minor child, to be videotaped and cable cast regarding this course.

Permission is hereby granted by:

Parent or Guardian Signature: _____

Printed Name: _____

Participant's Name: _____

Participant's Printed Name: _____

Date: _____

This release must be received prior to the final event.

Figure 6.4. Teen Top Models Fashion Course Participant Sign-In Sheet

Teen Top Models Fashion Course
Participant Sign-In Sheet

Date: _____

Name	Age	Phone #	E-mail Address

Stalder, Erika and Ariel Krietzman. 2008. *Fashion 101: A Crash Course in Clothing*. San Francisco: Zest Books.

Thompson, Lisa. 2007. *Trendsetter: Have You Got What It Takes to Be a Fashion Designer?* Minneapolis: Compass Point Books.

Vogt, Peter. 2007. *Career Opportunities in the Fashion Industry*. New York: Checkmark Books.

Step 7: Set Up the Program Area

Set up the meeting room with chairs. Keep an area clear of chairs for runway training. Set up sound equipment for music. Prepare sign-in table for taking roll. Set up book display areas.

Step 8: Conduct the Event

Begin with welcomes and housekeeping announcements. Introduce the speaker, and give an overview of what the session's agenda will be. Let the presenter conduct the program, but stay in the room to assist and interact with the teens.

Step 9: Evaluate the Program

Evaluations are helpful for planning future programs. Customize the evaluation form from Part I (see Figure I.3 on CD) for participants to fill out. Collect the forms as the audience leaves.

7
TERM PAPER CLINIC

PROGRAM DESCRIPTION

Teens learn to write a successful term paper with step-by-step plans illustrated in a Power-Point presentation. The presentation can be posted on your teen Web page, presented in a classroom or recreation center, as well as in the library. The clinic will help prepare students for state tests (e.g., in Texas, the TAKS).

PROGRAM GOALS

The library works in partnership with schools to teach students how to write successful term papers. The clinic helps students and teachers reduce stress by showing teens how to organize their research. This program supports teens with love, care, and attention (Developmental Assets® #1–6) and nurtures in them a commitment to learning (Developmental Assets #21–25).

HOW TO DO IT

Step 1: Make a Plan

To make the clinic timely, contact schools to find out when writing assignments are scheduled. Repeat the clinic throughout the school year to reach students when they have writing assignments.

Step 2: Set a Date, Book a Space

The one-hour Term Paper Clinic can be held on a Saturday or in the evening after school throughout the school year. Coordinate presentation times with outside agencies if presenting offsite.

The Term Paper Clinic can be held in a meeting room. The clinic can also be taken on the road to locations outside the library, such as schools, community centers, and Boys & Girls Clubs.

Step 3: Book the Presenter

The teen specialist designs and presents the lesson. Volunteers from the library personnel help to staff the classes in the library. Teachers will help when the clinic is presented in a classroom.

Step 4: Create a Program Format and Agenda

- Welcome, announcements, and introductions
- PowerPoint presentation

- Questions and answers
- End of session

The step-by-step topics to be covered in the PowerPoint presentation include the following:

- Understand Your Term Paper Assignment
- Choosing a Topic
- Limiting Your Topic
- Developing a Thesis Statement
- Verify Topic with Instructor
- Conducting Preliminary Research
- Preparing Bibliography and Footnotes
- In-Depth Research Strategies
- Writing the First Draft
- Revising the Paper—Draft #2
- Typing or Word Processing
- The Final Paper
- Web Sites About Term Papers

Step 5: Market the Program

Contact schools, community centers, Boys & Girls Clubs, homeschoolers' associations, and other youth organizations and distribute flyers (see Figure 7.1) throughout the community and in the library.

Step 6: Gather Materials, Prepare Handouts

Create a sign-in sheet (see Figure 7.2). Adapt the Term Paper Clinic PowerPoint presentation (on the accompanying CD and shown in Figure 7.3), and create a handout of the Web sites referenced in the PowerPoint presentation.

Book List

Coyle, William and Joe Law. 2007. *Research Papers*. New York: Pearson.

Davis, Harold. 2005. *Building Research Tools with Google for Dummies*. New York: Wiley.

Lenburg, Jeff. 2005. *The Facts on File Guide to Research*. New York: Facts on File.

Mann, Thomas. 2005. *The Oxford Guide to Library Research*. New York: Oxford University Press.

Natavi Guides. 2005. *Tackling the College Paper*. New York: Prentice Hall Press/Penguin Group.

Rozakis, Laurie. 2007. *Schaum's Quick Guide to Writing Great Research Papers*. New York: McGraw-Hill.

Shaw, Maura D. 2007. *Mastering Online Research: A Comprehensive Guide to Effective and Efficient Search Strategies*. Cincinnati: Writers Digest Books.

Sloan, Amy E. 2006. *Basic Legal Research: Tools and Strategies*. New York: Aspen Publishers.

Spalding, Cathy. 2005. *The Everything Guide to Writing Research Papers*. Avon, MA: Adams Media.

Stafford, Susan H. 2007. *Research Papers Unzipped*. Lawrenceville, NJ: Peterson's.

Terban, Marvin. 2007. *Ready! Set! Research! Your Fast and Fun Guide to Writing Research Papers That Rock!* New York: Scholastic.

Figure 7.1. Term Paper Clinic Publicity Flyer

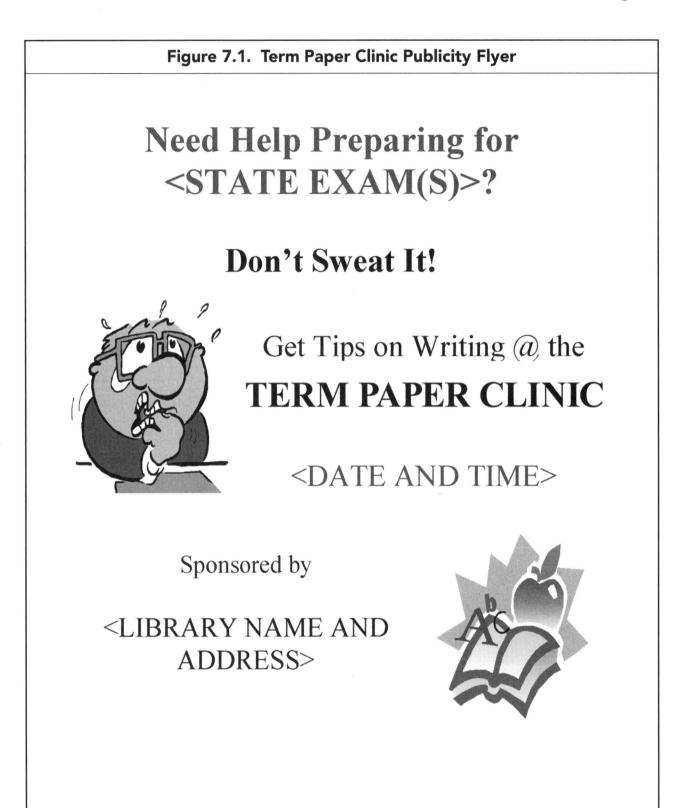

Figure 7.2. Term Paper Clinic Participant Sign-In Sheet			
Term Paper Clinic Participant Sign-In Sheet Date: _____			
Name	**Age**	**Grade**	**Phone #**

Figure 7.3. Term Paper Clinic PowerPoint Presentation

(Cont'd.)

Figure 7.3. Term Paper Clinic PowerPoint Presentation *(Continued)*

Understand Your Term Paper Assignment

Understand its *Purpose*, the *Length* of the paper, the *Type* of paper-- argumentative or narrative, the *Limits* in which you must confine your subject, and the *Due Date*.

Choosing A Topic

Select a topic in which you have a strong interest, curiosity, experience, or knowledge.

Topic Example:
"What are some of the mysteries that surround the death of American Presidents?"

Limiting Your Topic

Select a topic in which INFORMATION IS READILY AVAILABLE.

Limited Topic Example:
"What are some of the mysteries surrounding the death of President Lincoln?"

Developing a Thesis Statement

What do you intend to describe, prove, or analyze?

Thesis Statement Example:
"This paper is to point out some of the mysteries surrounding the tragic death of President Lincoln."

Verify Topic With Instructor

Review your thesis statement.

List reference books, indexes, periodicals, and other aids.

Conducting Preliminary Research

Make sure information and data on your chosen subject can be located readily.

General Reference Examples:

Encyclopedia Britannica
Gale Database
New Lincoln Library Encyclopedia
New Standard Dictionary
World Book Encyclopedia

(Cont'd.)

Figure 7.3. Term Paper Clinic PowerPoint Presentation *(Continued)*

Preparing Bibliography and Footnotes

Develop a preliminary bibliography

Author's Name; Title of Reference; Place of Publication; Name of Publisher; Date of publication; Comments (optional)

one reference per card

Footnote Example:

Current, Richard N., Mr. Lincoln, N.Y.: Dodd, Mead and Co., 1957. (see page - 382- Lincoln expresses his feelings about his own safety against would-be assassins.)

In-Depth Research Strategies

Select the sources most relevant to your subject.

Use various indexes, catalogs, or computer databases to locate books, articles, & documents.

Evaluate Information

for its accuracy and objectivity.

Note - Taking

Develop an orderly, systematic routine for note-taking.

Place only one idea on each card.

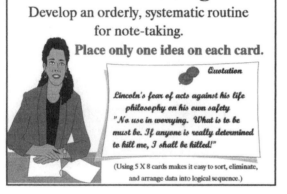

Quotation

Lincoln's fear of acts against his life philosophy on his own safety "No use in worrying. What is to be must be. If anyone is really determined to kill me, I shall be killed!"

(Using 5 X 8 cards makes it easy to sort, eliminate, and arrange data into logical sequence.)

Organizing the Paper

Create an outline. Determine main points. Select supporting evidence and examples.

Outline Example:

Lincoln's Assassination--An Unsolved Mystery

I. The act itself
II. Grant's strange behavior
III. Mrs. Lincoln's unfortunate choice of bodyguard
IV. The President's premonition
V. Booth's strange revelations

Writing the First Draft

Get down on paper a complete version of your topic.

First Draft Example:

Booth's decision to kill the President may have resulted from Lincoln stating, that he hoped that the freed slaves would be given the right to vote.// When Booth heard this, he threatened out loud.//

Mark you sources. Maintain an objective point of view.

Revising the Paper - Draft #2

Fill in missing information and references

Revised Example:

Booth's decision to kill the President may have resulted from Lincoln's statement of April 12, that he (Lincoln) hoped that the freed slaves of Louisiana would be given the right to vote.[7] Kelly remarked that when Booth heard of this, he fumed loudly and said, "Now, by God, I'll put him through![8]

[7] During the closing days of the war in 1865.
[8] Kelly, The Crime, p.4.

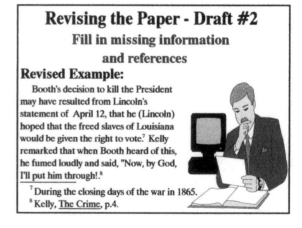

(Cont'd.)

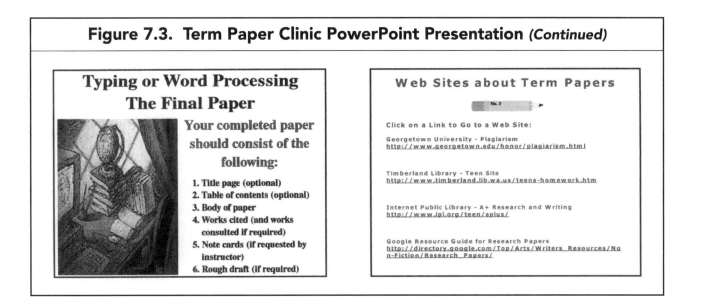

Figure 7.3. Term Paper Clinic PowerPoint Presentation *(Continued)*

Step 7: Set Up the Program Area

Set up tables and chairs. Set up laptop and projector. Be prepared with flip chart, if desired. Have paper and pencils on hand for note-taking. Create a book display.

Step 8: Conduct the Event

Welcome the audience; make announcements and introductions. Show the PowerPoint presentation. Leave time for questions and answers.

Step 9: Evaluate the Program

Evaluations are helpful for planning future programs. Customize the evaluation form from Part I (see Figure I.3 on CD) for participants to fill out. Collect the forms as the audience leaves.

Chapter 2

IN CONCERT: MUSIC CONCERTS AND SERIES

8
BROWN BAG CONCERTS
@ THE LIBRARY

PROGRAM DESCRIPTION

Patrons can stop by the library with a brown bag lunch to hear student ensemble performances twice a month.

PROGRAM GOALS

The Brown Bag Concerts give the library an opportunity to work in partnership with the schools to showcase student bands, choirs, orchestras, and ensembles. The concerts entice people into the library during lunch time so they become aware of its many resources. This program supports teens with love, care, and attention (Developmental Assets® #1–6), empowers them with opportunities to make a difference in their family and community (Developmental Assets #7–10), helps teens find activities that make constructive use of their time (Developmental Assets #17–20), and nurtures, celebrates, and affirms their positive identity (Developmental Assets #37–40).

HOW TO DO IT

Step 1: Make a Plan

Contact the director of choral music and the director of instrumental music at the schools and arrange a meeting to coordinate the concert series. Once you have the school music directors on board, take the funding proposal (for example, see Figure 8.1) to the director of a community arts organization to request funds to pay for bus transportation and lunch for participating students. Plan a lunch for the performing students. Our students had pizza and drinks.

Step 2: Set a Date, Book a Space

Concerts can be scheduled as frequently as your number of performers will accommodate. Our concerts were held twice a month, on the first and third Wednesdays of the month, November through mid May, from 12:00 noon to 1:00 p.m. No concerts were held during holidays and vacations or on test dates.

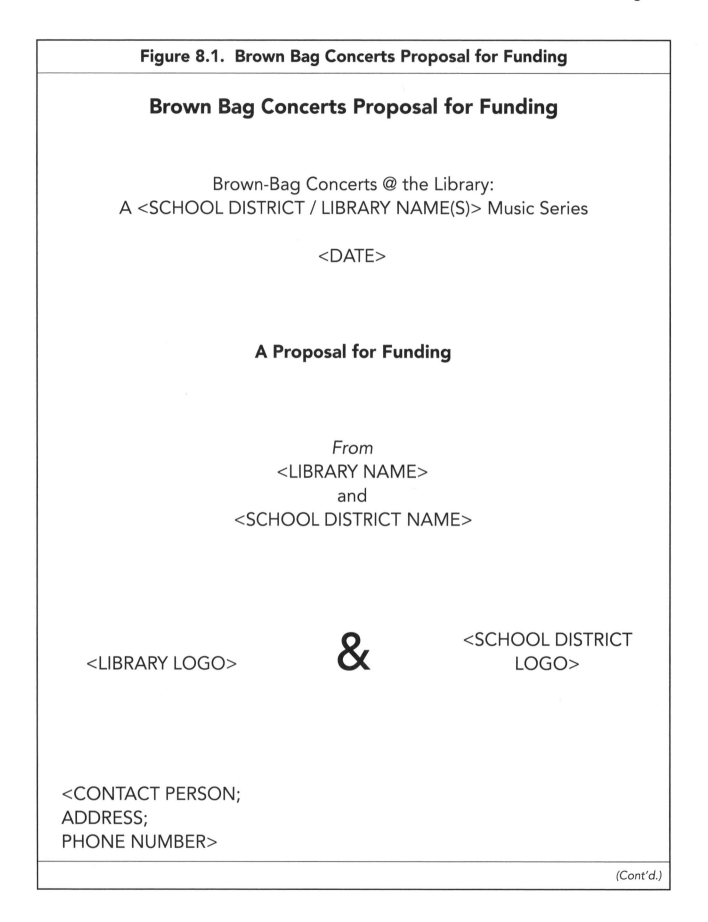

Figure 8.1. Brown Bag Concerts Proposal for Funding

Brown Bag Concerts Proposal for Funding

Brown-Bag Concerts @ the Library:
A <SCHOOL DISTRICT / LIBRARY NAME(S)> Music Series

<DATE>

A Proposal for Funding

From
<LIBRARY NAME>
and
<SCHOOL DISTRICT NAME>

<LIBRARY LOGO>   **&**   <SCHOOL DISTRICT LOGO>

<CONTACT PERSON;
ADDRESS;
PHONE NUMBER>

(Cont'd.)

Figure 8.1. Brown Bag Concerts Proposal for Funding *(Continued)*

Dear Friends and Supporters:

Research studies have shown that the Arts—music, dance, theatre, and the visual arts—are a vital component of a child's education from birth through secondary school. The studies have proven that the Fine Arts build brains and improve academic skills; teach work ethic and life skills; and enhance the school climate for students. Studies also show that students who participate in arts programs are more likely to become successful in whatever field of endeavor they choose. These patterns hold true for students from less privileged socioeconomic backgrounds as well. The arts reach all learners.

In partnership with <SCHOOL DISTRICT NAME>, the <LIBRARY NAME> is committed to providing quality and innovative services that enhance the community's appreciation and utilization of the library as an educational and cultural institution. Therefore, we request your participation in a special project to increase the community's awareness of the Fine Arts abilities of <SCHOOL DISTRICT NAME> students by showcasing their musical talent in a live public setting. These programs will provide students with outstanding Fine Arts experiences through the opportunities offered by local community arts organizations.

Each year approximately 1,000 students drop out of school. Search Institute® has identified 40 Developmental Assets® as building blocks of healthy development in young people. "Reading for Pleasure" is one of them. With this information in mind, the <LIBRARY NAME> is striving to find more ways to get young people actively involved in the library, in turn helping to reduce the drop-out rate. By having the opportunity to perform at the library, students will see it as a more user-friendly place. The library will furnish library card applications to ensure that all participating students who live within the city limits of <CITY/STATE> have library cards. This may encourage them to return to take advantage of the numerous resources available at the library. This may also persuade students to start "Reading [more] for Pleasure."

Proposed dates: <TIME FRAME> (excluding holidays, vacations, and test dates)
Grant request: <DOLLAR AMOUNT>
Title of the program: "Brown Bag Concerts @ the Library: A <SCHOOL DISTRICT / LIBRARY
                      NAMES> Music Series"
Sponsored by: <SCHOOL DISTRICT / LIBRARY NAMES>

Contacts: <LIBRARY CONTACT PERSON;
            ADDRESS;
            PHONE;
            E-MAIL ADDRESS>

            <SCHOOL DISTRICT CONTACT PERSON;
            ADDRESS;
            PHONE;
            E-MAIL ADDRESS>

            <ALTERNATE CONTACT PERSON;
            ADDRESS;
            PHONE;
            E-MAIL ADDRESS>

(Cont'd.)

Figure 8.1. Brown Bag Concerts Proposal for Funding (Continued)

The purpose of this program, "Brown Bag Concerts @ the Library," is twofold: to provide a means to showcase local student bands, choirs, etc.; and to provide an incentive to entice the downtown community into the library so they may be made aware of its many resources. This will offer an opportunity for all district schools to be recognized by participating in this ground-breaking effort. There are <NUMBER> high schools, each having <NUMBER> ensembles. The total number of performances for the year would be <NUMBER RANGE>. The funding will cover transportation expenses and promotion cost.

The Brown Bag Concerts will be held in the <BUILDING>, <ADDRESS>, once a week on <WEEKDAYs>, <TIME FRAME>. Members of the audience may bring their lunch (brown bag) or purchase a lunch from a local restaurant vendor. The event will be advertised using flyers and rave cards that will be distributed to all the local businesses in the area as well as to all of the high schools. A press release and public service announcement will be sent to local newspapers and radio and television stations. There will be no admission fee for the event. The schools' various ensembles will be booked in advance, so the students can notify their parents and relatives of the date they expect to perform. The library will provide a display of books, CDs, and other items that may be of interest. The event will also offer the opportunity to sign up for a library card.

BUDGET:

Categories	Cost
Bus Transportation	$
Student Lunches	$
Advertisement	$
Total cost for the year	$

"The arts are an instrumental part of a balanced education that provides both children and adults with a lifetime of benefits that are equally critical to community growth and development" (ArtGives.Org).

We would greatly appreciate the support of your organization in helping the <LIBRARY NAME> and <SCHOOL DISTRICT NAME> to implement this landmark endeavor. This music series will get not only more students involved in the library but the rest of the family as well. The school district and the public library are both working to help students develop the 40 Developmental Assets that allow young people to grow up healthy, caring, and responsible. We would like to thank you for joining in our efforts by considering this proposal.

Sincerely,

<CONTACT NAME;
AFFILIATION;
E-MAIL ADDRESS>

Live music will sound better in a larger space. Our Brown Bag Concerts took place in the Gallery area of the Central Library of the Fort Worth Public Library. Summer concerts can take place on the library lawn. The audience will bring their brown bag lunches. The library can provide beverages, if enough funds are acquired.

Step 3: Book the Presenters

Send a letter to the schools (for example, see Figure 8.2) to invite students to perform at the library. Schedule each student's and group's performances, and arrange transportation with the schools.

Step 4: Create a Program Format and Agenda

Noon	Welcome, announcements, and introduction of school ensembles
12:05	Student performance
12:30	End of concert
12:40	Students eat lunch
1:10	Students return to school

Step 5: Market the Program

Produce flyers and rave cards (see examples in Figures 8.3 and 8.4) to advertise the events, and distribute them throughout the school district. Send out a press release, and contact organizations such as the Chamber of Commerce, senior citizens groups, homeschoolers' organizations, and the courthouse (for jurors' lunch time activities). Distribute rave cards to local businesses and restaurants. Post flyers at daycare centers and apartment complexes. Invite downtown employees as well as parents for lunch at the library.

Step 6: Gather Materials

Create a display of appropriate books. Set up a poster or sign announcing the day's performers in advance to encourage attendance. Provide an adequate trash receptacle for leftover food and papers.

Book List

Bruser, Madeline. 1997. *The Art of Practicing: A Guide to Making Music from the Heart.* New York: Bell Tower.

Cefrey, Holly. 2003. *Backstage at a Music Video.* New York: Children's Press.

Dillon-Krass, Jacquelyn and Casimer B. Kriechbaum. 1978. *How to Design and Teach a Successful School String and Orchestra Program.* San Diego: Kjos West.

Eberts, Marjorie and Margaret Gisler. 2007. *Careers for Culture Lovers & Other Artsy Types.* New York: McGraw-Hill.

Hartocollis, Anemona. 2004. *Seven Days of Possibilities: One Teacher, 24 Kids, and the Music That Changed Their Lives Forever.* New York: Public Affairs.

J.G. Ferguson. 2004. *Careers in Focus: Art.* New York: Ferguson.

Lamp, Frederick. 2004. *See the Music, Hear the Dance: Rethinking African Art at the Baltimore Museum of Art.* New York: Prestel.

Sporborg, James Douglas. 1998. *Music in Every Classroom: A Resource Guide for Integrating Music Across the Curriculum, Grades K–8.* Englewood, CO: Libraries Unlimited.

Figure 8.2. Brown Bag Concerts Letter of Invitation to Schools

Brown Bag Concerts
Letter of Invitation to Schools

<LIBRARY LOGO>

<DATE>

Dear School Friends:

In partnership with <SCHOOL DISTRICT NAME>, the <LIBRARY NAME> is committed to increasing the community's awareness of the Fine Arts abilities of the district's students by showcasing their musical talent at the library in a live public setting, the "Brown-Bag Concerts @ the Library" music series. The purpose of this program is twofold: to provide a means to showcase <SCHOOL DISTRICT NAME> student bands, choirs, etc.; and to provide an incentive to entice people downtown into the library so they may be made aware of its many resources.

We appreciate your participation in this special project. Therefore, we would like to thank you by ensuring that all participating students who live within the city limits of <CITY/STATE> have library cards. For all those students who do not have cards, we will furnish library card applications. After getting parent signatures, please have them returned to you, the band/choir director. Once I receive the application back I will deliver the new cards to you. Because what the students are doing is considered "volunteer services," for those students who already have cards but may have an outstanding fine, we will reduce it or clear it completely so they can start using their cards again.

We are dedicated to providing quality and innovative services that enhance the community's appreciation and utilization of the library as an educational and cultural institution. For that reason we invite your students to use the <LIBRARY NAME> by owning their own Library Card.

Sincerely,

<CONTACT PERSON;
AFFILIATION;
ADDRESS;
PHONE NUMBER>

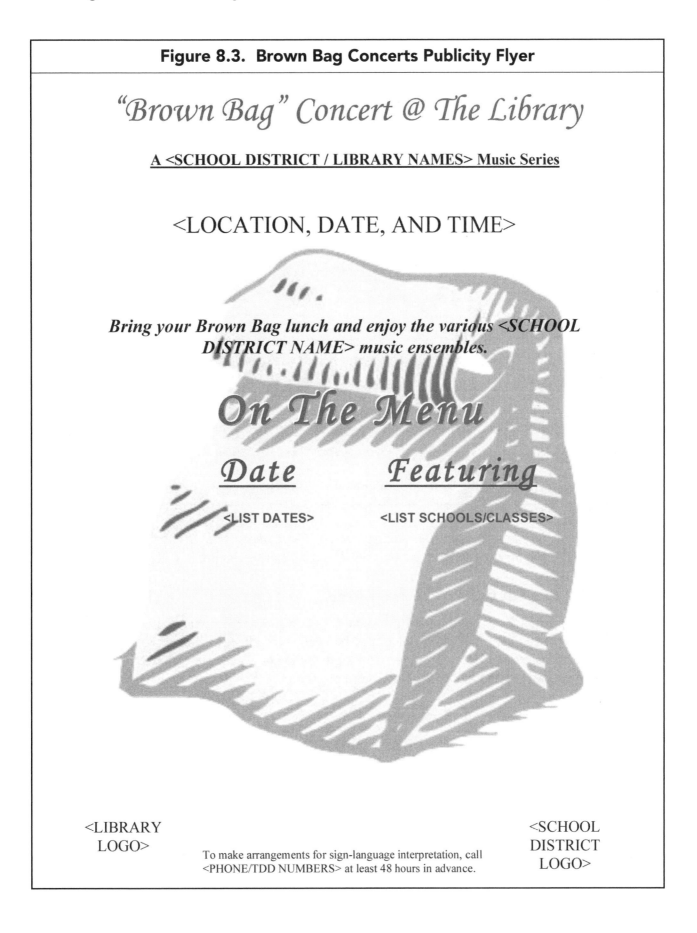

Figure 8.3. Brown Bag Concerts Publicity Flyer

"Brown Bag" Concert @ The Library

A <SCHOOL DISTRICT / LIBRARY NAMES> Music Series

<LOCATION, DATE, AND TIME>

Bring your Brown Bag lunch and enjoy the various <SCHOOL DISTRICT NAME> music ensembles.

On The Menu

Date | *Featuring*

<LIST DATES> | <LIST SCHOOLS/CLASSES>

<LIBRARY LOGO>

<SCHOOL DISTRICT LOGO>

To make arrangements for sign-language interpretation, call <PHONE/TDD NUMBERS> at least 48 hours in advance.

Figure 8.4. Brown Bag Concerts Rave Card

Vogel, Frederic B. and Ben Hodges. 2006. *The Commercial Theater Institute Guide to Producing Plays and Musicals.* New York: Applause Theatre & Cinema Books.

Step 7: Set Up the Program Area

Set up chairs for performers and audience. Set up audio equipment, including any speakers, amplifiers, and microphones that may be needed. Students will bring instruments, music, and music stands. Prepare a place for students to eat lunch after the concert. Set up book displays and handouts promoting future programs.

Step 8: Conduct the Event

Introduce the day's performers, including the students' names, the name of the performing group, and the home school. Lead the audience in applause after each performance. At the end of the concert, thank everyone for coming, and invite them to the next concert.

Step 9: Evaluate the Program

Evaluations are helpful for planning future programs. Customize the evaluation form from Part I (see Figure I.3 on CD) for participants to fill out. Collect the forms as the audience leaves.

9
CARAVAN OF JAZZ
@ THE LIBRARY

PROGRAM DESCRIPTION

A Caravan of Jazz event is a concert/lecture series in the library with local jazz artists. This program introduces teens to the world of jazz. A concert and lecture series would work equally well with a bluegrass, pop, emo, country western, folk, or an ethnic music theme that may be of particular interest in your community.

PROGRAM GOALS

A music program like the Caravan of Jazz attracts the youth and their families into the library, where they can be introduced to the many library resources that can help youth stay in school. The series educates area youth about the music industry and fosters an interest in all aspects of the music industry. It provides teenagers a tangible and intriguing opportunity for experiencing real music, played by real musicians in a live setting and at an extremely high performance level. With the teaching of the arts in many public schools being on the decline, the library offers a place to learn and enjoy music on a higher, more professional level. This program supports teens with love, care, and attention (Developmental Assets® #1–6), empowers them with opportunities to make a difference in their family and community (Developmental Assets #7–10), establishes clear boundaries and has high expectations (Developmental Assets #11–16), nurtures in them a commitment to learning (Developmental Assets #21–25), and helps teens develop life skills and social competencies (Developmental Assets #32–36).

HOW TO DO IT

Step 1: Make a Plan

Establish a relationship with a professional musician or music agent to assist you in making contacts in the music world. They can help you solicit on-air personalities as well as recording artists to host and participate in the event. They can conduct the interview segment to open up questions and answers with the audience.

They may also be able to help you obtain sponsorship. Many items are optional in this series, and all the costs are negotiable. For example, although the cost for artist fees, audio and video production, equipment rental, host gratuity, and production is about $3,600 for three months, all our program expenses were taken care of by the Rigsby Entertainment Group and by the local jazz radio station, Smooth Jazz Radio Station 107.5 FM, both of which responded favorably to our request for funds (see Figure 9.1).

Figure 9.1. Caravan of Jazz Concerts Proposal for Funding

Caravan of Jazz Concerts
Proposal for Funding

<DATE>

Dear <CONTACT PERSON>:

The <LIBRARY NAME> has a history of successful innovative programming, including annual music-related events (symposiums, concerts, talent shows, etc.) at the library that feature panels of experts from the field of music. We would like to continue our efforts so that teens will progress not only in school but also in their dreams of becoming musicians. Therefore, we request your participation in a <DOLLAR AMOUNT> special project to educate young adults and teach them how to appreciate the contemporary art form of music.

<RADIO STATION> has been committed to providing quality and innovative programs that enhance the community's appreciation of live jazz, featuring local artists. Your past demonstration of dedication to the community through sponsorship of local music events encourages us to turn to <RADIO STATION> for its support in order to augment music education for the youth of <CITY/STATE> by hosting Caravan of Jazz @ the Library, Concert/Lecture Series.

Statistics show that approximately 1,000 students drop out of school each year. The Search Institute® has identified 40 Developmental Assets® that are building blocks of healthy development in young people, one of which is "Reading for Pleasure." With this information in mind, the <LIBRARY NAME> is continuing to strive to find ways to get more young people actively involved with the library, in turn helping to reduce the drop-out rate.

The purpose of this program, the Caravan of Jazz @ the Library, is twofold: to educate youth, of which a high percentage are disadvantaged, about the music industry; and to provide an incentive to entice them into the library so they may take advantage of its many resources, thereby encouraging them to stay in school. The <LIBRARY NAME>, along with assistance and guidance from <PERFORMANCE CURATOR>, is hosting this concert/lecture series to foster an interest in all aspects of the music industry. This series is a way to introduce teens to the world of jazz. It will allow teenagers a tangible and intriguing opportunity for experiencing real music, played by real musicians in a live setting and at an extremely high performance level.

Proposed dates: <TIME FRAME>
Grant request: <DOLLAR AMOUNT>
Title of the program: "Caravan of Jazz @ the Library: A Concert/Lecture Series"
Sponsored by: <LIBRARY NAME>

Contact:

<LIBRARY CONTACT PERSON;
ADDRESS AND PHONE>

(Cont'd.)

Figure 9.1. Caravan of Jazz Concerts Proposal for Funding (Continued)

This program, Caravan of Jazz @ the Library, is planned for teenagers along with their entire families who live in and around the <CITY/STATE> area. It was designed by <PERFORMANCE CURATOR> to provide a means to heighten teen interest in jazz and other music genres. This program will also provide an avenue to bring musicians back in touch with their audience. On-air personalities and recording artists will host the event and also conduct the interview segment, which will open up questions and answers with the audience. This will offer an opportunity for national recording and touring artists to participate in this groundbreaking effort. We will film each event to create a DVD history of this series for the continuing education of music students from grade school level to college and for musicians wanting to find out what's going on in <CITY/STATE>. This provides a documentary resource for the artists' who live and work here and also for the wealth of touring artists' who perform in our area. The funding will cover the operating expense.

The Caravan of Jazz will be held in the <LOCATION>, <WEEKDAYs>, <TIME FRAME>. The event will be advertised using flyers and rave cards that will be distributed to all the local high schools in the area as well as local businesses. A press release and public service announcement will be sent to local newspapers and radio and television stations. There will be seating for approximately <NUMBER> with no entrance fee into the event. The artists will be booked in advance. The library will provide the facility and advertising. The library will also provide a display of books, CDs, and other items concerning the music industry.

BUDGET:

Categories	Cost
Artist Fee	$
Audio & Video Production	$
Equipment Rental	$
Host Gratuity	$
Production Cost	$_____
Total	$
Total cost for three (3) months	$_____

We would greatly appreciate the support of <RADIO STATION> in helping the <LIBRARY NAME> implement this groundbreaking effort. This music series will get not only more teenagers involved in the library but the rest of the family as well. With the teaching of the arts in public schools being on the decline, the library will be able to provide a "safe house" for learning and enjoying music on a higher, more professional level. The city, the school district, and the public library are all working to help teenagers develop the 40 Developmental Assets that help young people grow up healthy, caring, and responsible. The <LIBRARY NAME> would like to thank <RADIO STATION> for joining in our efforts by considering this proposal.

Sincerely,

<CONTACT PERSON;
AFFILIATION;
E-MAIL ADDRESS>

Step 2: Set a Date, Book a Space

Try a summer evening for your concert series. Our Caravan of Jazz concert/lecture series was held every first Monday of the month, from 6:00 to 8:00 p.m., June through August.

A large space is needed for the music performance to accommodate a staging area and the audience. If your library has a suitable lawn or outdoor facilities, you might hold the concerts outdoors.

Step 3: Book the Presenters

Contact a local performing artist or agent to act as the Performance Curator. His or her job will be to contact and schedule performers.

Step 4: Create a Program Format and Agenda

6:00	View video of past performances
6:30	Welcome and showtime
7:15	Question and answer
7:35	Final set
8:00	Closing remarks

Step 5: Market the Program

Produce rave cards and flyers (for examples, see Figures 9.2 and 9.3) to advertise, and ask the Teen Advisory Board to distribute them to the schools and other places where teens hang out. Send out a press release announcing the series. Contact various youth organizations such as the Boys & Girls Clubs. Distribute rave cards to local businesses. Post flyers at restaurants.

Step 6: Gather Materials

Assemble appropriate books to display during the concerts.

Book List

Anderson, Iain. 2007. *This Is Our Music: Free Jazz, the Sixties, and American Culture.* Philadelphia: University of Pennsylvania Press.

Bolden, Tonya. 2007. *Take-off: American All-Girl Bands During WWII.* New York: Alfred A. Knopf.

Cook, Richard and Brian Morton. 2006. *The Penguin Guide to Jazz Recordings.* London: Penguin.

Dell, Pamela. 2005. *Miles Davis: Jazz Master.* Chanhassen, MN: Child's World.

Elish, Dan. 2005. *Louis Armstrong and the Jazz Age.* New York: Children's Press.

Holmes, Thom. 2006. *Jazz.* New York: Facts on File.

Isoardi, Steven Louis. 2006. *The Dark Tree: Jazz and the Community Arts in Los Angeles.* Berkeley: University of California Press.

Kahn, Ashley. 2006. *The House That Trane Built: The Story of Impulse Records.* New York: W.W. Norton & Co.

Lydon, Michael. 2007. *How to Play Classic Jazz Guitar: Six Swinging Strings.* New York: Routledge.

Figure 9.2. Caravan of Jazz Concerts Rave Card

Figure 9.3. Caravan of Jazz Concerts Publicity Flyer

<LIBRARY NAME> and
<PERFORMANCE
CURATOR>

"Caravan of Jazz
@ The Library"
Concert/Lecture Series

Guest Hosts:
<LIST NAMES>

<ARTIST PHOTO>

<LOCATION>
<LIBRARY ADDRESS>

<DATE>
<SHOWTIMES>

EXECUTIVE PRODUCER: <PERFORMANCE CURATOR>
SUPERVISING PRODUCER: <LIBRARY CONTACT PERSON;
CONTACT INFORMATION>

<ARTIST PHOTO>

<LIBRARY
LOGO>

To make arrangements for sign-language interpretation, call
<PHONE/TDD NUMBERS> at least 48 hours in advance.

Ratliff, Ben. 2007. *Coltrane: The Story of a Sound*. New York: Farrar, Straus and Giroux.
Schoeneberger, Megan. 2005. *Ella Fitzgerald: First Lady of Jazz*. Mankato, MN: Capstone Press.
Tanner, L.E. 2006. *The Jazz Image: Masters of Jazz Photography*. New York: Abrams.
Winter, Jonah and Sean Qualls, illus. 2006. *Dizzy*. New York: Arthur A. Levine Books.

Step 7: Set Up the Program Area

Set up sound equipment. Set up video equipment.

Step 8: Conduct the Event

Welcome the audience, thank the sponsors, and introduce the performers. Lead the audience in applause after each performance.

Step 9: Evaluate the Program

Evaluations are helpful for planning future programs. Customize the evaluation form from Part I (see Figure I.3 on CD) for participants to fill out. Collect the forms as the audience leaves.

10
BOOK CLUB & JAM SESSION
@ THE LIBRARY

PROGRAM DESCRIPTION

Celebrate Jazz Appreciation Month by combining a book club discussion and a jam session in a nightclub setting at the library. Like the Caravan of Jazz concert, this music program can easily be adapted to the favored music in your community.

PROGRAM GOALS

April is Jazz Appreciation Month. A jazz celebration at the library will foster an interest in the music industry, introduce teens to the world of jazz, and invite the youth and their families into the library so they may take advantage of its many resources. Any music genre-themed program will allow teenagers and their families an opportunity to experience real music, played by real musicians, while listening to a book talk given by a real author. This program supports teens with love, care, and attention (Developmental Assets® #1–6), establishes clear boundaries and has high expectations (Developmental Assets #11–16), nurtures in teens a commitment to learning (Developmental Assets #21–25), and helps them develop life skills and social competencies (Developmental Assets #32–36).

HOW TO DO IT

Step 1: Make a Plan

The Teen Advisory Board as well as volunteers from the library personnel can staff the event. Ask a jazz station radio personality to emcee the session. The room can be set up as a nightclub scene with round tables and a book display on jazz music as a centerpiece on each table. Serve easy refreshments like popcorn and sodas. Jazz music will be performed by a jazz band. Local jazz artists from the audience who have their own instruments will be allowed to sit in with the band, as in a jam session. A local author will do a book talk, and a storyteller will tell stories about jazz icons. Invite local book clubs as special guests. Members can RSVP to reserve a table. Coordinate your available authors and musicians for a themed program.

To promote library card sign-ups, admission is free to library card holders. Offer a door prize drawing if funds permit. Contact Wal-Mart, write a grant, or contact another good funding resource for community events to pay for the band, refreshments, and a door prize. Our Wal-Mart provided a $50.00 gift card as a door prize.

Step 2: Set a Date, Book a Space

April is Jazz Appreciation Month and the ideal time for the jazz version of this program. Our event took place on a Sunday from 3:00 to 5:00 p.m.

A meeting room or community room will work well. Limit the number of reservations to the number of seats you can accommodate around the tables, leaving a stage area for the presenters.

Step 3: Book the Presenters

Contact a local author to do the book talk portion of the program. Book a local band for the event. Contact a storyteller to tell stories about music icons. For example, author and professor Michael Meckna, of Texas Christian University, led our book talk on his book *Satchmo: The Louis Armstrong Encyclopedia*, the featured band was State of Mind, and our storyteller was DeeCee Cornish.

Step 4: Create a Program Format and Agenda

2:00	Jazz music
2:15	Welcome and showtime
2:30	Book review
3:10	Jazz music
3:40	Stories of past performers
4:20	Jazz music
4:40	Door prize drawing and closing remarks
4:50	Final set
5:00	Closing

Step 5: Market the Program

Produce rave cards and promotional flyers (see Figures 10.1 and 10.2) for the Teen Advisory Board to distribute to appropriate places. Send out a press release (see Figure 10.3). Contact various youth organizations such as the Boys & Girls Clubs. Send invitation letters to local book clubs and other supporters (see Figure 10.4). Distribute rave cards to local businesses, and post flyers at restaurants.

Step 6: Gather Materials

Create a menu (see Figure 10.5) on a poster to hang by the refreshment table.

Book List

Brothers, Thomas David. 2006. *Louis Armstrong's New Orleans*. New York: W.W. Norton.

Dell, Pamela. 2005. *Miles Davis: Jazz Master*. Chanhassen, MN: Child's World.

Elish, Dan. 2005. *Louis Armstrong and the Jazz Age*. New York: Children's Press.

Ford, Carin T. 2008. *Duke Ellington: "I Live with Music."* Berkeley Heights, NJ: Enslow.

Gourse, Leslie and Martin French. 2007. *Sophisticated Ladies: The Great Women of Jazz*. New York: Dutton Children's Books.

Holmes, Thom. 2006. *Jazz*. New York: Facts on File.

Kahn, Ashley. 2006. *The House That Trane Built: The Story of Impulse Records*. New York: W.W. Norton & Co.

Oliphant, Dave. 2007. *Jazz Mavericks of the Lone Star State*. Austin: University of Texas Press.

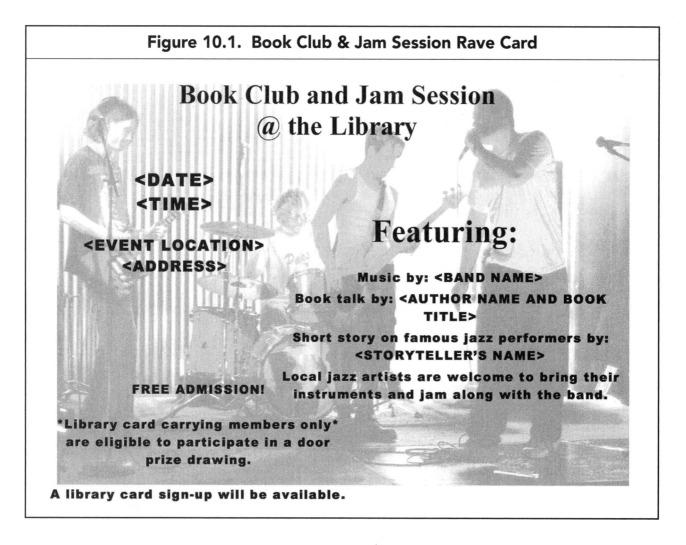

Figure 10.1. Book Club & Jam Session Rave Card

Parker, Robert Andrew. 2008. *Piano Starts Here: The Young Art Tatum*. New York: Schwartz & Wade Books.

Ratliff, Ben. 2007. *Coltrane: The Story of a Sound*. New York: Farrar, Straus and Giroux.

Schoeneberger, Megan. 2005. *Ella Fitzgerald: First Lady of Jazz*. Mankato, MN: Capstone Press.

Tanner, L.E. 2006. *The Jazz Image: Masters of Jazz Photography*. New York: Abrams.

Winter, Jonah and Sean Qualls, illus. 2006. *Dizzy*. New York: Arthur A. Levine Books.

Step 7: Set Up the Program Area

Set up the meeting room like a night club with small round tables and a bar for refreshments. If your library doesn't own small tables, borrow or rent them from a church or wedding reception facility. Set up sound equipment. Set up a refreshment table or bar.

Step 8: Conduct the Event

Welcome the audience, and introduce the emcee. Stay in the room to help host, serve refreshments, and take care of any problems. Lead the audience in applause, and thank the performers and the audience for coming.

Figure 10.2. Book Club & Jam Session Publicity Flyer

Figure 10.3. Book Club & Jam Session Press Release

Book Club & Jam Session
Press Release

<LIBRARY NAME>
NEWS RELEASE
FOR IMMEDIATE RELEASE
<DATE>

CONTACT:
<CONTACT NAME AND TITLE>
<LIBRARY NAME AND ADDRESS>
<PHONE NUMBER>
<E-MAIL ADDRESS>

Don't You Wanta Jam?

Calling all book clubs and book lovers! This is your chance to read, write, and jam! April is National Jazz Appreciation Month, and at the <LIBRARY NAME> the 3Rs stand for Read, Rite, and Rock. We invite you to help us celebrate the occasion with a *Book Club & Jam Session*, <WEEKDAY>, <DATE>, from <TIME FRAME>, at <EVENT LOCATION AND ADDRESS>.

The <EVENT LOCATION> will be staged as a "Night Club" with round tables and book displays on jazz, topped off with a musical centerpiece. Complimentary popcorn and soft drinks will be served.

Our jam session will feature local jazz band <BAND NAME>. If you play an instrument, bring it along. Sit in with the band. As our special guests, book club members will attend on a book talk with <AUTHOR NAME>, who will discuss <HIS/HER> book <BOOK TITLE>. As an added bonus, storyteller <NAME> will wow the crowd with a lively tale on famous jazz artists.

Seating is limited, so we ask that book clubs RSVP. The program is free and open to the public. *Only Library Card Carrying Members* will be able to participate in the door prize drawing. There will be a library card sign-up table at this event. For more information, contact <NAME, PHONE NUMBER, AND E-MAIL>.

<CONTACT NAME AND TITLE>
<LIBRARY NAME AND ADDRESS>
<PHONE NUMBER>
<E-MAIL ADDRESS>

Figure 10.4. Letter of Invitation to the Book Club & Jam Session

Letter of Invitation to the Book Club & Jam Session

<LIBRARY LOGO>

<DATE>

Calling all book clubs! This is your chance to read, write, and jam!

April is National Jazz Appreciation Month, and the <LIBRARY NAME> invites you to help us celebrate with a *Book Club & Jam Session*, <WEEKDAY>, <DATE>, from <TIME FRAME>, <EVENT LOCATION>.

The <EVENT LOCATION> will be staged as a "Night Club" with author <AUTHOR NAME>, who will discuss <HIS/HER> book, <BOOK TITLE>. As an added bonus, storyteller <NAME> will wow the crowd with a lively tale on famous jazz artists.

Seating is limited with six participants per table. We are asking book clubs to RSVP. The program is free and open to the public. *Only Library Card Carrying Members* will be able to participate in the door prize drawing. There will be a library card sign-up table at this event. For more information, contact <NAME, PHONE NUMBER, AND E-MAIL>.

Sincerely,

<CONTACT NAME AND TITLE>
<LIBRARY NAME AND ADDRESS>
<PHONE NUMBER>
<E-MAIL ADDRESS>

Figure 10.5. Book Club & Jam Session Bar Menu

Book Club & Jam Session Bar Menu

~~Rum &~~ Coke	Free
~~Gin &~~ 7 Up	Free
~~Whisky &~~ Water	Free
Root Beer	Free
Popcorn	Free

Step 9: Evaluate the Program

Evaluations are helpful for planning future programs. Customize the evaluation form from Part I (see Figure I.3 on CD) for participants to fill out. Collect the forms as the audience leaves.

11
YOUTH GOSPEL FEST

PROGRAM DESCRIPTION

Invite surrounding churches and organizations to participate in a gospel music festival featuring youth choirs, praise teams, performance groups, dance teams, and solo artists to celebrate National Black History Month.

PROGRAM GOALS

The Youth Gospel Fest is a good opportunity for the library to showcase talented young people, make connections with local churches and other organizations that work with young people, and make families aware of the many religious and inspirational resources available at the library. This program supports teens with love, care, and attention (Developmental Assets® #1–6), empowers them with opportunities to make a difference in their family and community (Developmental Assets #7–10), helps teens find activities that make constructive use of their time (Developmental Assets #17–20), helps them develop life skills and social competencies (Developmental Assets #32–36), and nurtures, celebrates, and affirms their positive identity (Developmental Assets #37–40).

HOW TO DO IT

Step 1: Make a Plan

Invite area church and other teen music ensembles to perform. Open the program to the public with free admission. A grant can pay for refreshments. Volunteers from the library staff as well as Teen Advisory Board members can host the event. The Youth Gospel Fest, held during National Black History Month, will give tribute to the Black Church and the "Old Negro Spirituals" for the important role they played in the struggle toward freedom.

Step 2: Set a Date, Book a Space

Hold the event in February during National Black History Month. Plan about three hours for the event, depending on how many performers register. If your library has Sunday hours, a Sunday afternoon works well to attract families.

Step 3: Book the Presenters

Send out letters of invitation (see Figure 11.1) and applications (see Figure 11.2) to churches and youth groups early in January or sooner. Address the letters to youth organization directors and church youth group leaders. Each group and solo performer must complete the application form to participate.

Figure 11.1. Letter of Invitation to the Youth Gospel Fest

Letter of Invitation·
to the Youth Gospel Fest

<LIBRARY LOGO>

<DATE>

<CONTACT NAME>
<CHURCH/YOUTH GROUP NAME>
<ADDRESS>

Dear <CONTACT NAME>:

The <LIBRARY NAME> is in the process of planning major events during Black History Month this year and would like your assistance. We are planning a Youth Gospel Fest to be held at <EVENT LOCATION> on <WEEKDAY>, <DATE>, from <TIME FRAME>. We need your help to create a memorable event.

We would like church and youth groups to participate in this activity at our library. The youth choirs and youth praise teams from the churches in the <CITY/STATE> area are invited to the Youth Gospel Fest. The event will be held in <EVENT LOCATION>, which can accommodate <NUMBER> people. The event will also include exhibits by local African-American artists, creating a unique cultural experience for our local youth during Black History Month.

Rules and regulations will be sent at a later date; entry forms are enclosed. Entry and admittance to the event will be free to the public.
Any questions, suggestions, or recommendations should be directed to:

<CONTACT NAME>
<PHONE NUMBER>
<E-MAIL ADDRESS>

Sincerely,

<CONTACT NAME AND TITLE>
<LIBRARY NAME>
<ADDRESS>
<PHONE NUMBER>

Figure 11.2. Application to Participate in the Youth Gospel Fest

Application to Participate
in the Youth Gospel Fest

<LIBRARY LOGO>

Name of Church: _____

Address of Church: _____

_____

Phone number @ Church: _____

Web page and e-mail address: _____

_____

Name of Organization or Group: _____

Brief description of Group submitting application: _____

_____

_____

_____

_____

Contact person: _____

    Phone number: _____

    E-mail address: _____

Please return applications to:
<CONTACT NAME>
<LIBRARY NAME>
<ADDRESS>

Step 4: Create a Program Format and Agenda

2:00	Welcome, announcements, and introductions
2:05	Program: local choirs, praise dancers, spoken word poetry, Christian rappers, and soloists
4:00	Closing remarks
4:05	Reception
5:00	End of program

Step 5: Market the Program

Produce flyers (see Figures 11.3 and 11.4) to advertise the event, and distribute them to churches, youth organizations, schools, Boys & Girls Clubs, and homeschoolers' organizations. Post flyers at various teen hot spots and centers.

Step 6: Gather Materials

Assemble books for display during the concert.

Book List

Carpenter, Bil. 2005. *Uncloudy Days: The Gospel Music Encyclopedia*. San Francisco: Backbeat Books.

Darden, Bob. 2004. *People Get Ready! A New History of Black Gospel Music*. New York: Continuum.

Gaither, Bill and Jerry B. Jenkins. 1997. *Homecoming: The Story of Southern Gospel Music Through the Eyes of Its Best-Loved Performers*. Grand Rapids, MI: Zondervan.

Hand, Edie and Buddy Killen. 2006. *A Country Music Christmas: Christmas Songs, Memories, Family Photographs, and Recipes from America's Favorite Country and Gospel Stars*. New York: Broadway Books.

Jones, Bobby and Les Sussman. 2000. *Make a Joyful Noise: My 25 Years in Gospel Music*. New York: St. Martin's Press.

Orgill, Roxane. 2002. *Mahalia: A Life in Gospel Music*. Cambridge, MA: Candlewick Press.

Walker, James L., Jr. 2008. *This Business of Urban Music: A Practical Guide to Achieving Success in the Industry, from Gospel to Funk to R&B to Hip-Hop*. New York: Billboard Books.

Werner, Craig Hansen. 2004. *Higher Ground: Stevie Wonder, Aretha Franklin, Curtis Mayfield, and the Rise and Fall of American Soul*. New York: Crown Publishers.

Woog, Adam. 2006. *The History of Gospel Music*. San Diego, CA: Lucent Books.

Zolten, J. Jerome. 2003. *Great God A'mighty! The Dixie Hummingbirds: Celebrating the Rise of Soul Gospel Music*. New York: Oxford University Press.

Step 7: Set Up the Program Area

Set up chairs for the audience and participants. Set up sound equipment, and create a stage area for the performers. Prepare a place for refreshments.

Figure 11.3. Youth Gospel Fest Publicity Flyer

Source: Designed by "D" Metcalf.

Figure 11.4. Youth Gospel Fest Publicity Poster

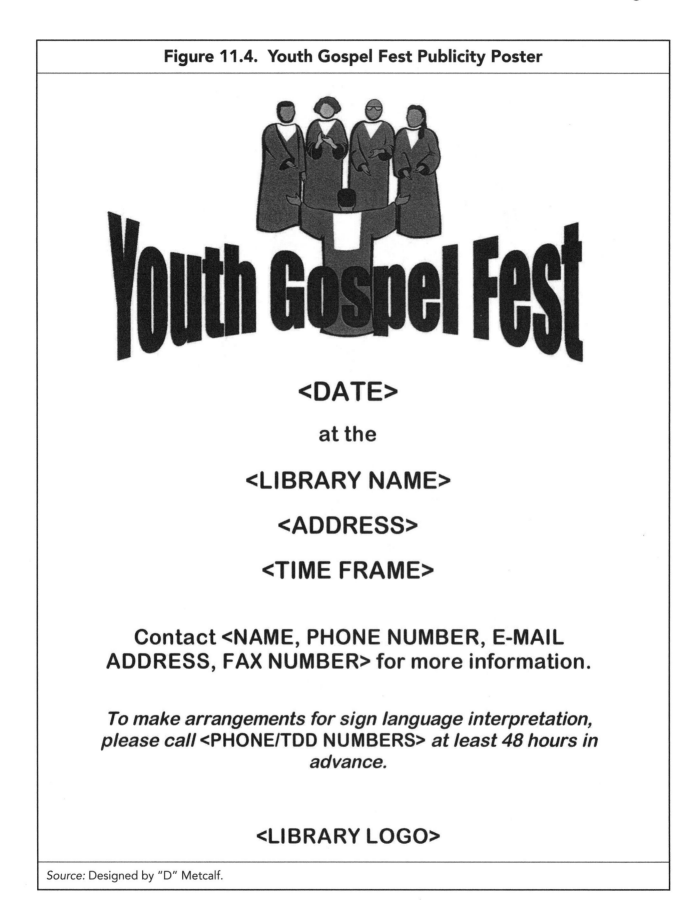

<DATE>

at the

<LIBRARY NAME>

<ADDRESS>

<TIME FRAME>

Contact **<NAME, PHONE NUMBER, E-MAIL
ADDRESS, FAX NUMBER>** for more information.

*To make arrangements for sign language interpretation,
please call **<PHONE/TDD NUMBERS>** at least 48 hours in
advance.*

<LIBRARY LOGO>

Source: Designed by "D" Metcalf.

Step 8: Conduct the Event

Welcome the performers and the audience. Make housekeeping announcements (restrooms, refreshments), and introduce the first performer. Lead the audience in applause at the end of each performance. At the end, thank everyone for coming to the program.

Step 9: Evaluate the Program

Evaluations are helpful for planning future programs. Customize the evaluation form from Part I (see Figure I.3 on CD) for participants to fill out. Collect the forms as the audience leaves.

12
HIP-HOP SYMPOSIUM

PROGRAM DESCRIPTION

Today hip-hop is not just music; it is a culture. The Hip-Hop Symposium includes a panel discussion with industry professionals, a live DJ, live performances, an open-mic session, and vendors featuring hip-hop paraphernalia. This program is an opportunity for aspiring artists to submit music demos and photographs to representatives from local talent agencies and record labels.

Music is a strong influence in the lives of young people. Spotlight the collection and services of the library to show teens the business side of the hip-hop industry. The Hip-Hop Symposium shows teens that there are more ways to make it in the business than just singing, dancing, and rapping.

PROGRAM GOALS

The Hip-Hop Symposium will spotlight collections and services of the library to generate an enthusiasm for reading and will attract teens to the library for an experience that will encourage self-expression. The event is a learning experience for the entire family, teaching young people the business side of the hip-hop industry. This program supports teens with love, care, and attention (Developmental Assets® #1–6), empowers them with opportunities to make a difference in their family and community (Developmental Assets #7–10), establishes clear boundaries and has high expectations (Developmental Assets #11–16), instills positive values to guide them (Developmental Assets #26–31), and helps them develop life skills and social competencies (Developmental Assets #32–36).

HOW TO DO IT

Step 1: Make a Plan

The symposium includes a panel discussion made up of industry professionals. Call and arrange meetings with an entertainment attorney, a record label representative, a recording studio representative, a fashion designer, a music artist, a producer, a songwriter, a radio personality, and a librarian. Discuss the program idea and panel discussion with them.

Offer vendors a booth if they contribute a door prize. Arrange to invite a DJ and spoken word artists, and plan to include an open-mic session.

Request funds to pay for a DJ, sound equipment, and refreshments. The Teen Advisory Board (TAB), library staff, and parents of TAB members can staff the symposium. Patrons can attend for free with a library card, and be sure to offer library card sign-ups at the door.

Step 2: Set a Date, Book a Space

The symposium can be scheduled on a Saturday afternoon. The program is four hours long. Vendors may start setting up in the morning. Several rooms are used, each for a different part of the symposium.

Step 3: Book the Presenters

Send letters of invitation and registration and release forms to the schools (see Figures 12.1, 12.2, and 12.3). Send letters of invitation and participation forms to vendors (see Figures 12.4 and 12.5), panelists (see Figures 12.6 and 12.7), and record companies (see Figure 12.8).

Step 4: Create a Program Format and Agenda

This agenda shows the timing and order of the program as it was presented at our library. Customize the agenda to fit the number of performers you have.

12:50	Music	DJ
1:00	Welcome	TAB members
1:05	Black National Anthem	
1:10	Introduction of moderators	Teen librarian and organizers
1:15	Panel discussion	
2:30	Presentations and announcements	Teen librarian and organizers
2:45	Break (check out an item to receive a ticket for a prize drawing)	
3:15	Live entertainment	
4:30	Open-mic session	
4:45	Door prize drawing	
5:00	Close	

Step 5: Market the Program

Send out a press release (see Figure 12.9). Produce flyers and rave cards (see Figures 12.10 and 12.11) to advertise the event, and distribute them to the schools, Boys & Girls Clubs, community centers, the YWCA, and so forth. Ask TAB members to distribute rave cards to places where teens hang out.

Step 6: Gather Materials

Assemble books for a display. Create sign-in sheets for panelists, entertainers, and vendors (see Figures 12.12, 12.13, and 12.14). To further promote the library's resources, create a listing of key books on various aspects of the music business (see Figure 12.15).

Figure 12.1. Hip-Hop Symposium Letter of Invitation to Teens

Hip-Hop Symposium
Letter of Invitation to Teens

<DATE>

Dear Hip-Hop Teen Talent Participant:

Well it's about that time of year again—February, Black History Month, and the annual Hip-Hop Symposium. The <LIBRARY NAME>, in collaboration with <CO-HOST NAME(S)>, will present our annual Hip-Hop Symposium, "Lean Back in <YEAR>," as we continue to reach out to teens in an effort to promote education, self-expression, and self-esteem.

Your participation is so very important. Please keep in mind that foul language and/or obscene gestures are inappropriate in the library. The purpose of this unique event is to show young people the business side of the hip-hop industry by spotlighting the collection and services of the library, in turn generating an enthusiasm for reading among the youth of <CITY/STATE>. As always, the symposium will include a panel discussion with industry professionals, a live DJ, live performances, an "open-mic" session, and vendors featuring hip-hop paraphernalia. This event is an opportunity for aspiring artists to meet, as well as submit music demos and photographs to, representatives from local talent agencies and record labels. There will be door prizes and refreshments. You must have a library card to be eligible for the drawings. A library card sign-up will be available at the door. The card is free.

The Hip-Hop Symposium will be <WEEKDAY>, <DATE>, from <TIME FRAME> in <EVENT LOCATION>. The library will open at <TIME>. Please arrive no later than <TIME>, for check-in. Admission to the event is free. I am enclosing a few rave cards so you can help us to promote the event by inviting a few of your friends or other young people you may know. If you need more cards please contact me.

We are looking forward to your participation in our annual Hip-Hop Symposium, "Lean Back in <YEAR>" because your presence will make a difference. Many thanks in advance!

Sincerely,

<CONTACT NAME AND TITLE>
<LIBRARY NAME AND ADDRESS>
<PHONE NUMBER>
<E-MAIL ADDRESS>

Figure 12.2. Hip-Hop Symposium Open-Mic Registration Form for Teens

Hip-Hop Symposium
Open-Mic Registration Form for Teens

Name: _____ Age: _____

Address: _____

City: _____ State: _____ Zip: _____

Phone: _____ E-mail: _____

Grade: _____ School: _____

Performance Number: _____

- -

Name: _____ Age: _____

Address: _____

City: _____ State: _____ Zip: _____

Phone: _____ E-mail: _____

Grade: _____ School: _____

Performance Number: _____

- -

Name: _____ Age: _____

Address: _____

City: _____ State: _____ Zip: _____

Phone: _____ E-mail: _____

Grade: _____ School: _____

Performance Number: _____

- -

Figure 12.3. Hip-Hop Symposium Teen Participant Information and Release Form

Hip-Hop Symposium Teen Participant Information and Release Form

Name of individual or group: _____

Age(s) of participant(s): _____

Managing company: _____

Contact person: _____

Address: _____

City: _____ State: _____ Zip: _____

Phone: _____ E-mail: _____

Preferred contact method: _____

Length and type of act (acts should not exceed 7 minutes):

_____

_____

Brief bio of individual or group (attach additional sheet if necessary):

_____

_____

_____

_____

Minor participants must have their parent's or guardian's permission. Therefore, each member of the group must turn in a release form with appropriate signatures (see next page).

Thank you for your time! *Please return this sheet by* <DATE> to: <LIBRARY NAME AND ADDRESS>, *or by fax to* <FAX NUMBER>. *If you need additional information, please contact* <CONTACT NAME, PHONE NUMBER, AND E-MAIL ADDRESS>.

Forms not received by the requested time will result in cancellation.

(Cont'd.)

Figure 12.3. Hip-Hop Symposium Teen Participant Information and Release Form *(Continued)*

Each participant must have a release form on file; therefore, you may make as many copies of this sheet as needed.

Permission / Release Form:

Permission is hereby granted for the library to use my name, likeness, and photograph, or the name, likeness, and photograph of a minor child, regarding the *Hip-Hop Symposium* for editorial, public relations, promotional, and advertising purposes on behalf of the <LIBRARY NAME>.

Permission is also hereby granted for the use of my image and/or voice, or the image and/or voice of a minor child, to be videotaped and cable cast regarding this event.

Permission is hereby granted by:

Parent or Guardian Signature: _____

Printed Name: _____

Participant's Name: _____

Participant's Printed Name: _____

Date: _____

This release must be received prior to performing.

**Figure 12.4. Hip-Hop Symposium Letter of Invitation
to Vendors and Record Companies**

Hip-Hop Symposium Letter of Invitation to Vendors and Record Companies

<DATE>

Dear Hip-Hop Vendors / Record Labels:

Well it's about that time of year again—February, Black History Month, and the annual Hip-Hop Symposium. The <LIBRARY NAME>, in collaboration with <CO-HOST NAME(S)>, will present our annual Hip-Hop Symposium, "Lean Back in <YEAR>," as we continue to reach out to teens in an effort to promote education, self-expression, and self-esteem.

Your participation is so very important. Please keep in mind that the purpose of this unique event is to show young people the business side of the hip-hop industry by spotlighting the collection and services of the library, in turn generating an enthusiasm for reading among the youth of <CITY/STATE>. As always the symposium will include a panel discussion with industry professionals, a live DJ, live performances, an "open-mic" session (if time permits), and vendors featuring hip-hop paraphernalia. This event is an opportunity for aspiring artists to meet, as well as submit music demos and photographs to, representatives from local talent agencies and record labels. There will be door prizes and refreshments. A library card is required to be eligible for the drawings. A library card sign-up will be available at the door. The card is free.

The Hip-Hop Symposium will be <WEEKDAY>, <DATE>, from <TIME FRAME> in <EVENT LOCATION>. The library will open at <TIME>. Vendors may start setting up at that time. Please arrive no later than <TIME>, so you can check in and submit your door prize contribution. Admission to the event is free. I am enclosing a few rave cards so you can help us to promote the event by inviting a few of your colleagues or young people you know. If you need more cards please contact me.

We are looking forward to your participation in our annual Hip-Hop Symposium, "Lean Back in <YEAR>" because your presence will make a difference. Many thanks in advance!

Sincerely,

<CONTACT NAME AND TITLE>
<LIBRARY NAME AND ADDRESS>
<PHONE NUMBER>
<E-MAIL ADDRESS>

Figure 12.5. Hip-Hop Symposium Vendor Booth Registration Form

Hip-Hop Symposium
Vendor Booth Registration Form

Name of business or organization: _____

Representative's name: _____

Address: _____

City: _____ State: _____ Zip: _____

Phone: _____ E-mail: _____

Preferred contact method: _____

Type of products (attach additional sheet if necessary):

_____

_____

_____

Item(s) to be donated to the symposium as a "give away"*:

_____

_____

Special needs (tables, chairs, electricity, etc.):

_____

_____

Symposium starts at <TIME>. Booth setup time from <TIME FRAME> day of event.

*Donated items for "give away" must be submitted prior to setup.

Thank you for your time! Please return this sheet by <DATE> to: <LIBRARY NAME AND ADDRESS>, or by fax to <FAX NUMBER>. If you need additional information please contact <CONTACT NAME, PHONE NUMBER, AND E-MAIL ADDRESS>.

Forms not received by the requested time will result in cancellation.

Figure 12.6. Hip-Hop Symposium Letter of Invitation to Panelists

Hip-Hip Symposium
Letter of Invitation to Panelists

<DATE>

Dear Hip-Hop Panelist:

Well it's about that time of year again—February, Black History Month, and the annual Hip-Hop Symposium. The <LIBRARY NAME>, in collaboration with <CO-HOST NAME(S)>, will present our annual Hip-Hop Symposium, "Lean Back in <YEAR>," as we continue to reach out to teens in an effort to promote education, self-expression, and self-esteem.

Your participation is so very important. Please keep in mind that the purpose of this unique event is to show young people the business side of the hip-hop industry by spotlighting the collection and services of the library, in turn generating an enthusiasm for reading among the youth of <CITY/STATE>. As always the symposium will include a panel discussion with industry professionals, a live DJ, live performances, an "open- mic" session (if time permits), and vendors featuring hip-hop paraphernalia. This event is an opportunity for aspiring artists to meet, as well as submit music demos and photographs to, representatives from local talent agencies and record labels. There will be door prizes and refreshments. A library card is required to be eligible for the drawings. A library card sign-up will be available at the door. The card is free.

The Hip-Hop Symposium will be <WEEKDAY>, <DATE>, from <TIME FRAME> in <EVENT LOCATION>. The library will open at <TIME>. Vendors may start setting up at that time. Please arrive no later than <TIME>, so you can check in and submit your door prize contribution. Admission to the event is free. I am enclosing a few rave cards so you can help us to promote the event by inviting a few of your colleagues or young people you know. If you need more cards please contact me.

We are looking forward to your participation in our annual Hip-Hop Symposium, "Lean Back in <YEAR>" because your presence will make a difference. Many thanks in advance!

Sincerely,

<CONTACT NAME AND TITLE>
<LIBRARY NAME AND ADDRESS>
<PHONE NUMBER>
<E-MAIL ADDRESS>

Figure 12.7. Hip-Hop Symposium Panel Participant Information Form

Hip-Hop Symposium
Panel Participant Information Form

Name of company or organization: _____

Representative's name: _____

Position and/or title: _____

Address: _____

City: _____ State: _____ Zip: _____

Phone: _____ E-mail: _____

Preferred contact method: _____

Brief bio (attach additional sheet if necessary):

_____

_____

_____

_____

_____

_____

_____

_____

Thank you for your time! *Please return this sheet by* <DATE> to: <LIBRARY NAME AND ADDRESS>, or by fax to <FAX NUMBER>. If you need additional information please contact <CONTACT NAME, PHONE NUMBER, AND E-MAIL ADDRESS>.

Forms not received by the requested time will result in cancellation.

Figure 12.8. Hip-Hop Symposium Record Company Participant Information Form

Hip-Hop Symposium
Record Company Participation Information Form

Name of record label or recording studio: _____

Representative or contact person: _____

Address: _____

City: _____ State: _____ Zip: _____

Phone: _____ E-mail: _____

Preferred contact method: _____

Item(s) or studio time to be donated to the symposium as a "give away"*:

_____

_____

Special needs (tables, chairs, electricity, etc.):

_____

_____

_____

Brief company description (attach additional sheet if necessary):

_____

_____

_____

_____

Symposium starts at <TIME>. Booth *setup time* from <TIME FRAME> day of event.

*Donated Items for "give away" must be submitted prior to setup.

Thank you for your time! *Please return this sheet by* <DATE> to: <LIBRARY NAME AND ADDRESS>, or by fax to <FAX NUMBER>. If you need additional information please contact <CONTACT NAME, PHONE NUMBER, AND E-MAIL ADDRESS>.

Forms not received by the requested time will result in cancellation.

Figure 12.9. Hip-Hop Symposium Press Release

Hip-Hop Symposium Press Release

<LIBRARY NAME>
NEWS RELEASE
FOR IMMEDIATE RELEASE
<DATE>

CONTACT:
<CONTACT NAME AND TITLE>
<LIBRARY NAME AND ADDRESS>
<PHONE NUMBER>
<E-MAIL ADDRESS>

"LEAN BACK IN <YEAR>"
<LIBRARY NAME>
<n>th ANNUAL HIP-HOP SYMPOSIUM

The <LIBRARY NAME>, in collaboration with <CO-HOST(S) NAME(S)>, present the <n>th Annual Hip-Hop Symposium, "Lean Back in <YEAR>," as we continue to reach out to teens in an effort to promote education, self-expression, and self-esteem. This year we have added a new sponsor, <SPONSOR NAME>. The purpose of this unique event is to show young people the business side of the hip-hop industry by spotlighting the collection and services of the library, in turn generating an enthusiasm for reading among the youth of <CITY/STATE>. The symposium will include a panel discussion with industry professionals, a live DJ, models, live performances, a "free style" session, and vendors featuring hip-hop paraphernalia. There will be door prizes and an opportunity for aspiring artists to meet, as well as to submit music demos and photographs to, representatives from local talent agencies and record labels.

The Hip-Hop Symposium is scheduled for <WEEKDAY>, <DATE>, from <TIME FRAME>, in <EVENT LOCATION>. Vendors will start setting up at <TIME>. The cost of a booth is the contribution of a door prize. Admission to the event is free with the showing of a library card. Library card sign-up will be available at the door.

Figure 12.10. Hip-Hop Symposium Publicity Flyer

"Lean Back in <YEAR>"

Open Free Style

Vendor Booths

Annual Hip Hop Symposium

Door Prizes

Submit Demos

<DATE>
<TIME FRAME>
<LIBRARY NAME AND ADDRESS>

Free Admission w/ Library Card

Live Entertainment

Panel of Industry Experts

<LIBRARY LOGO>

To make arrangements for sign language interpretation, please call <PHONE/TDD NUMBERS>, at least 48 hours in advance.

Figure 12.11. Hip-Hop Symposium Rave Card

FRONT

BACK

Figure 12.12. Hip-Hop Symposium Panelist Sign-In Sheet			
Hip-Hop Symposium **Panelist Sign-In Sheet** Date: _____			
Organization/Company	**Representative**	**Title**	**Phone #**

Figure 12.13. Hip-Hop Symposium Teen Talent Sign-In Sheet

Hip-Hop Symposium
Teen Talent Sign-In Sheet

Date: _____

Name of Group/Individual	Contact Person	Phone #	E-mail Address

Figure 12.14. Hip-Hop Symposium Vendor Sign-In Sheet

Hip-Hop Symposium
Vendor Sign-In Sheet

Date: _____

Organization/Company	Representative	Phone #	Donation	E-mail Address

Figure 12.15. Listing of Key Library Books About the Music Industry

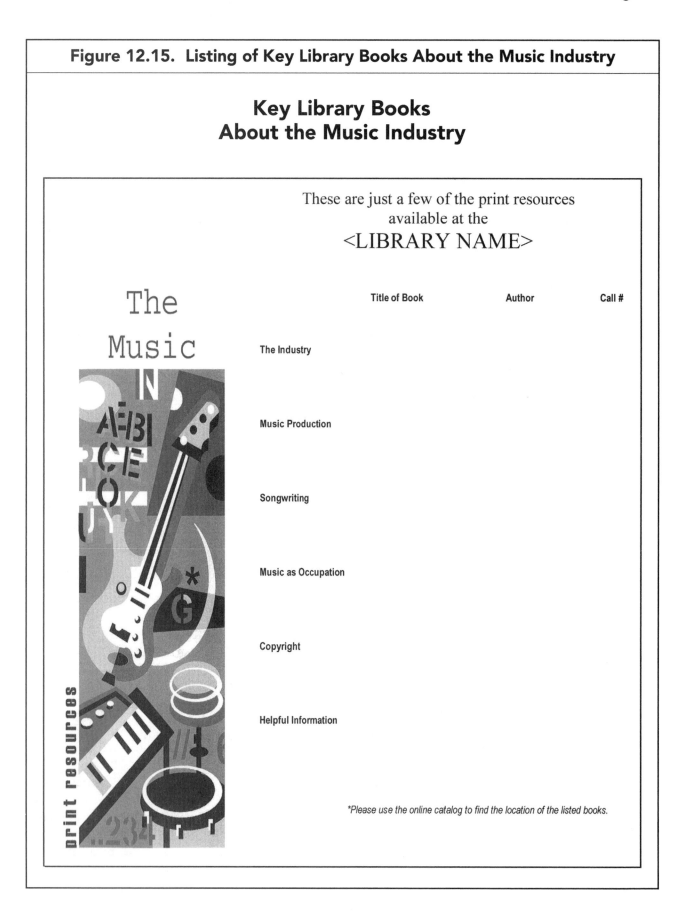

Key Library Books
About the Music Industry

These are just a few of the print resources
available at the
<LIBRARY NAME>

	Title of Book	Author	Call #
The Industry			
Music Production			
Songwriting			
Music as Occupation			
Copyright			
Helpful Information			

Please use the online catalog to find the location of the listed books.

Book List

Avalon, Moses. 2001. *Secrets of Negotiating a Recording Contract: The Musician's Guide to Understanding and Avoiding Sneaky Lawyer Tricks*. San Francisco: Backbeat Books.

Belleville, Nyree. 2000. *Booking, Promoting and Marketing Your Music: A Complete Guide for Bands and Solo Artists*. Vallejo, CA: MixBooks.

Brown, Ethan. 2005. *Queens Reigns Supreme: Fat Cat, 50 Cent and the Rise of the Hip-Hop Hustler*. New York: Anchor Books.

Coleman, Mark. 2003. *Playback: From the Victrola to MP3, 100 Years of Music, Machines, and Money*. New York: Da Capo Press.

Howard, George. 2004. *Getting Signed! An Insider's Guide to the Record Industry*. Boston: Berklee Press.

Kalmar, Veronika. 2002. *Label Launch: A Guide to Independent Record Recording, Promotion, and Distribution*. New York: St. Martin's Griffin.

Kennedy, Erica. 2004. *Bling*. New York: Miramax.

Koller, Fred. 2001. *How to Pitch and Promote Your Songs*. New York: Allworth Press.

Ro, Ronin. 2001. *Bad Boy: The Influence of Sean "Puffy" Combs on the Music Industry*. New York: Pocket Books.

Schaefer, A.R. and James Henke. 2004. *Making a First Recording*. Mankato, MN: Capstone High-Interest Books.

Schulenberg, Richard. 2005. *Legal Aspects of the Music Industry: An Insider's View*. New York: Billboard Books.

Schwartz, Daylle Deanna. 2002. *The Real Deal: How to Get Signed to a Record Label*. New York: Billboard Books.

Schwartz, Daylle Deanna. 2003. *Start & Run Your Own Record Label*. New York: Billboard Books.

Schwartz, Daylle Deanna. 2005. *I Don't Need a Record Deal! Your Survival Guide for the Indie Music Revolution*. New York: Billboard.

Thall, Peter M. 2002. *What They'll Never Tell You About the Music Business: The Myths, the Secrets, the Lies (& a Few Truths)*. New York: Watson-Guptill.

WetFeet.com. 2003. *The WetFeet Insider Guide to Careers in Entertainment & Sports*. San Francisco, CA: WetFeet.

Step 7: Set Up the Program Area

Set up a table and chairs in a stage area for the panelists. Set up chairs in auditorium style, or use an auditorium if you have one. Set up sound equipment. Set up tables and chairs in an adjacent area for the vendors. Set up tables and chairs in another room or area for the record companies and a table for refreshments. Set up a participant sign-in and library card sign-up table near the entrance of the auditorium, and set out brochures and sign-in sheets.

Step 8: Conduct the Event

Follow the prepared agenda.

Step 9: Evaluate the Program

Evaluations are helpful for planning future programs. Customize the evaluation form from Part I (see Figure I.3 on CD) for participants to fill out. Collect the forms as the audience leaves.

13
LIBRARY TEEN IDOL COMPETITION

PROGRAM DESCRIPTION

The Library Teen Idol Competition is a talent search contest that mimics the popular television show *American Idol*. Branch libraries hold auditions and send their winners to a semifinal competition at the main library. Professionals from the music industry serve as judges to determine which teen performers will be selected to appear in a final competition. The final competition takes place at the main library, and the audience votes for the winner. The Library Teen Idol receives a contract for free studio time to record a demo and performs at various library functions. Smaller libraries can adapt the same program idea and hold the entire competition in one day.

PROGRAM GOALS

The Library Teen Idol Competition gives teens the opportunity to share their talents and perform for an audience and judges. The program gives the library an opportunity to partner with local businesses and attract teens and their families to the library. Circulation of music-related library materials will increase with publicity and displays. To increase the number of library card holders, require participants to own a library card. The Teen Idol Competition supports teens with love, care, and attention (Developmental Assets® #1–6), establishes clear boundaries and high expectations (Developmental Assets #11–16), helps teens find activities that make constructive use of their time (Developmental Assets #17–20), and nurtures, celebrates, and affirms their positive identity (Developmental Assets #37–40).

HOW TO DO IT

Step 1: Make a Plan

Ask a recording studio to donate studio time for the winner. Request funds or write a grant for a DJ, approximately $150.00, and for refreshments, $25.00 to $50.00, depending on the expected attendance and choice of refreshments.

The auditions begin in the branch libraries six weeks before a scheduled semifinal competition. Each library branch will host an audition. Any branch with little or no room for auditions should make arrangements with a nearby facility. Ask music industry professionals to judge all of the branch auditions; include judges from a recording studio, a marketing company, a production company, a concert booking company, and record labels or similar professions in your community.

Contestants selected at the branch libraries audition again for a semifinal round at the main library before the judges only. The top seven contestants from the semifinal round are advanced to the grand finale also held at the main library. Rehearsal for the finale is held at the library during the week before the show. Invite a TV or radio personality to host the grand finale, and the audience will vote for the grand prize winner. Each branch receives ten tickets for the audience for the final judging. Branches may distribute the tickets any way they wish, such as by a drawing.

The winner can represent the library at other community functions and outings and receive free studio time and a free marketing and free promotions package compliments of the music professionals. Solicit prizes from local businesses for the runner-ups. Award each participant a Certificate of Appreciation from the library. Complete the program with a Meet the Contestants reception sponsored by a supportive community organization.

Smaller libraries can collaborate with other library systems to hold a similar competition or hold a one-day event. Hold auditions before the final event at the library to narrow down the number of final performers for the judging audience.

Step 2: Set a Date, Book a Space

Two dates are set for branch auditions, and each branch library selects a first and a second choice for a date and chooses a two-hour time slot on that date about six weeks before the grand finale. The schedule is filled on a first come, first served basis.

Step 3: Book the Presenter

The sample letter in Figure 13.1 provides information the judges will need. Send the competition rules (see Figure 13.2), admission tickets (see Figure 13.3), and teen registration forms (see Figure 13.4) to the branches.

Step 4: Create a Program Format and Agenda

This is the agenda that our library used for the Teen Idol Competition. Adapt it to your library's needs.

2:00	Music	Guest musician
2:10	Welcome/introductions	Teen Advisory Board
2:20	Opening performance	Guest musician
2:30	Competition begins	Teen idols
3:00	Return to stage	All contestants
3:05	Voting by the audience	
3:15	Performance	Guest musician
3:20	Presentation	Judges
3:30	Words of encouragement	Industry professionals
3:40	Performance	Guest band
4:00	Presentation of awards	Librarian
4:15	Closing remarks and door prizes	Librarian

Step 5: Market the Program

Announce a callout for participants over the radio and in the newspapers. Contestants must register in advance in order to participate. Produce flyers (Figure 13.5) to advertise the events and distribute to the schools, Boys & Girls Clubs, the YMCA, community centers,

Figure 13.1. Letter to the Judges of the Library Teen Idol Competition

Letter to the Judges of the Library
Teen Idol Competition

<LIBRARY LOGO>

<DATE>

Dear Judges of the Library Teen Idol Competition:

Listed below are the locations, dates, and times of the auditions to be held in the branches. Please respond by return e-mail, as soon as possible, to let me know which ones you or a representative from your organization can attend.

	Location	Date	Time	Phone #
1.				
2.				
3.				
4.				
5.				
6.				
7.				
8.				

Semifinals held at: <LOCATION>

Grand Finale held at: <LOCATION>

If you have any questions please contact <CONTACT NAME>, at <PHONE NUMBER AND E-MAIL ADDRESS>.

Figure 13.2. Library Teen Idol Competition Rules

Library Teen Idol Competition Rules

About Library Teen Idol

This is a talent search contest that mimics the television show *American Idol*. Initial auditions will be held throughout the <LIBRARY NAME> system. Professionals from the music industry will determine which performers will be selected to appear in a final competition at <LOCATION> in front of an audience. Judges will assess each act before the audience vote to determine the winner. The Library Idol will receive a contract for free studio time to record three tracks, at a cost of $1,500 per track, totaling $4,500, to make a demo. Other gifts will be given to the 1st and 2nd place runner-ups.

Auditions will begin in <MONTH>. Each library branch must submit a tentative schedule of the date and time their location would like to host an audition. Reservations will be filled on a first come, first served basis. If any conflicting dates occur, branches will be notified to reschedule. Schedules will be posted and publicized to recruit contestants. A semifinal competition will be held on <DATE> at <LOCATION> with contestants and judges only. The top seven contestants will advance to the Grand Finale that will also be held at <LOCATION>, <DATE>, where the audience will select the winner. To try to make the final judging by the audience fair, each branch will be given 10 admission tickets that they can give out at their discretion. That way no location will be over-represented.

I. Participants

1. Must be 13 to 19 years of age.
2. Must register in advance at any <LIBRARY NAME> Branch.
3. Can audition only once.
4. Must own a library card.
5. Only one song per participant—must not exceed 2 minutes in length.
6. Must provide your own CD/audio tape accompaniment or sing unaccompanied.

II. Registration

1. Teens wishing to participate in the Contest must first complete a Registration Form, containing their name, birth date, phone number, and e-mail address.
2. Participants must submit a Parent Permission Slip/Release Form along with the Registration Form in advance of auditioning to any branch location.
3. Library personnel and the contest organizers reserve the right to reject any Registration Form at their sole discretion.

(Cont'd.)

Figure 13.2. Library Teen Idol Competition Rules (Continued)

III. Contest Procedure

1. Over a period of six weeks, professionals from the music industry will hold auditions at the various library locations to select the teens who will compete for the title of <LIBRARY NAME> Teen Idol <YEAR>. Lyrics must be clean and appropriate.

2. At the end of the six weeks, the judging staff will compile a list of those eligible participants who will advance to the semifinal competition at <LOCATION>. Judges reserve the right to reject improper entries.

3. Seven finalists will be chosen at the semifinal competition to advance to the Grand Finale that will be held at <LOCATION> on <DATE>.

4. Judges' selection of the winning participants to compete at <LOCATION> shall be final and shall not be subject to objection or challenge. The selection of Branch Winners shall be at the sole discretion of the contest judges. Library staff reserve the right to disqualify or otherwise exclude from consideration any participant(s) for failing to abide by these rules or by local, state, or federal laws or ordinances.

5. Library personnel will post the name of each winner in each building as well as on the Web site after Branch Winners are selected. Each Branch Winner will be awarded a Library Idol Prize Pack that includes library merchandise and prizes provided by local sponsors. Participants are eligible to win only one Library Prize Pack during the term of the contest, and they maintain their eligibility to win the Grand Prize at the conclusion of the contest.

6. On the day of the final competition, the audience will select the Grand Prize Winner along with 1st and 2nd place runner-ups. Prizes will be awarded accordingly.

7. The contest is open to teens 13 years of age up to 19 years of age, except library employees and their immediate families.

8. This contest is not endorsed by or affiliated with the American Idol television program or the Fox Television Network/Twentieth Century Fox.

9. Entry and acceptance of prize constitute permission for <LIBRARY NAME> to use winner's entry, name, likeness, photograph, voice, and statements regarding this contest for editorial, public relations, promotional, and advertising purposes on behalf of the <LIBRARY NAME> without compensation unless prohibited by law.

10. Prizes are nontransferable. No substitutions or cash in lieu of prizes. The library reserves the right to substitute a prize of equal or greater value if any prize becomes unavailable for any reason.

11. Anyone participating and winning a prize releases the library, judges, any contest sponsors, their parents, affiliates, subsidiaries and agents, and their respective officers, directors, employees, and agents from any and all liability or responsibility for any claim arising in connection with participation in the contest or any prize awarded.

Figure 13.3. Library Teen Idol Admission Tickets to the Final Competition

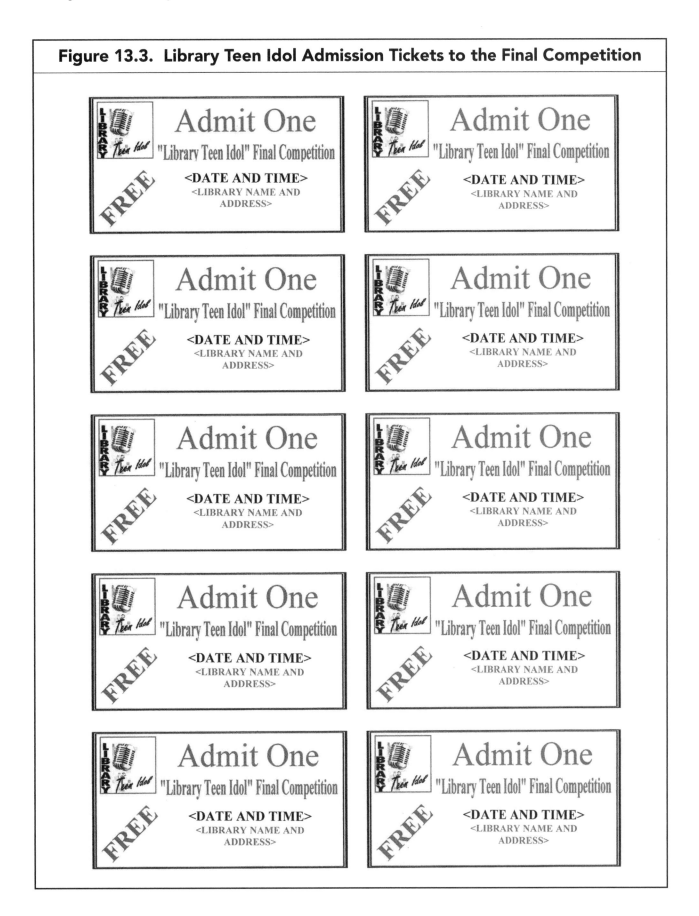

Figure 13.4. Library Teen Idol Contestant Registration Form

Library Teen Idol
Contestant Registration Form

Auditioning at: _____ Branch/Regional Library

Date of Audition: _____

Name: _____

Address: _____

Telephone Number: _____

Age: _____ Date of Birth: _____

Grade: _____ School: _____

E-mail Address: _____

Permission/Release Form:

Permission is hereby granted for the library to use my name, likeness, and photograph, or the name, likeness, and photograph of a minor child, regarding Library Teen Idol for editorial, public relations, promotional, and advertising purposes on behalf of the <LIBRARY NAME>.

Permission is also hereby granted for the use of my image and/or voice, or the image and/or voice of a minor child, to be videotaped and cable cast regarding this contest.

Permission is hereby granted by:

Parent or Guardian Signature: _____

Printed Name: _____

Participant's Name: _____

Participant's Printed Name: _____

Date: _____

This release must be received prior to the audition for the event.

Figure 13.5. Library Teen Idol Competition Publicity Flyer

**JOIN THE
COMPETITION!**
Grand prize includes
FREE STUDIO TIME

\<LIBRARY NAME\>
Is on a Hunt for Gifted Teens
Sign Up Now!

**There will be three rounds of competition
with the first starting soon at a library
branch near you!**

For registration information,
visit our Web site at \<WEB SITE ADDRESS\>
or go to your local branch library.

\<LIBRARY
LOGO\>

To make arrangements for sign-language interpretation, call
\<PHONE/TDD NUMBERS\> at least 48 hours in advance.

and other youth organizations. Ask Teen Advisory Board members to distribute them in places where teens hang out. Post information about the competition on the library's Web site (see Figure 13.6). Send out a press release (Figure 13.7) and Public Service Announcement publicizing the event and promoting the library. Write a follow-up story on the winner to further promote the library.

Step 6: Gather Materials

All library locations should build displays of books, videos, magazines, and other materials pertaining to the music industry. Create a teen sign-in sheet (see Figure 13.8) and performance roster (see Figure 13.9) for the day of the event. Create a performance rating form for the judges (see Figure 13.10), and provide pencils. Prepare letters to send to teens who are invited to the semifinals and grand finale and to send to the competition winner (see Figure 13.11). For the final competition, prepare voting ballots for the audience (see Figure 13.12) and a Certificate of Recognition for the winner (see Figure 13.13).

Book List

Brooks, Lonnie, Cub Koda, and Wayne Baker Brooks. 1998. *Blues for Dummies*. Foster City, CA: IDG Books Worldwide.

Deutsch, Jeffrey. 1998. *Teach Yourself to Read Music: A Guide for Pop, Rock, Blues and Jazz Singers*. Milwaukee: Houston.

Fulford, Phyllis and Michael Miller. 2003. *The Complete Idiot's Guide to Singing*. Indianapolis: Alpha Books.

Grant-Williams, Renée. 2003. *Vocal Master Class: With Renee Grant-Williams*. Nashville: Throat Patrol Video Products.

Guard, Rick. 2005. *Singing*. Chicago: Contemporary Books.

Lebon, Rachel L. 1999. *The Professional Vocalist: A Handbook for Commercial Singers and Teachers*. Lanham, MD: Scarecrow Press.

McElroy, Donna and Matthew Marvuglio. 2003. *Ultimate Practice Guide for Vocalists: Featuring Donna McElroy*. Boston: Berklee Press.

Pogue, David and Scott Speck. 1997. *Classical Music for Dummies*. New York: Harper Audio.

Rodgers, Janet B. 2002. *The Complete Voice & Speech Workout: The Documentation and Recording of an Oral Tradition for the Purpose of Training and Practices*. New York: Applause Theatre and Cinema Books.

Step 7: Set Up the Program Area

Set up the auditorium with a table for judges. Set up sound equipment. Prepare a sign-in table. Set up an area or meeting room with refreshments. Have voting ballots ready for the audience.

Step 8: Conduct the Event

Follow the prepared agenda.

Step 9: Evaluate the Program

Evaluations are helpful for planning future programs. Customize the evaluation form from Part I (see Figure I.3 on CD) for participants to fill out. Collect the forms as the audience leaves.

Figure 13.6. Library Teen Idol Competition Web Site Posting

Library Teen Idol Competition Web Site Posting

<LIBRARY LOGO>

It's not exactly *American Idol*, but it's close! Competition heats up this summer at the <LIBRARY NAME> with a Teen Idol contest. This talent search mimics the popular Fox Television Network show. The library is on a hunt for gifted teens, and one lucky youngster could grab the grand prize, which includes $4,500 worth of studio time. There are also prizes for the 1st and 2nd runner-ups.

There will be three rounds of competition with the first starting soon at a library branch near you! For directions to a specific library location and for registration information, contact <CONTACT NAME, PHONE NUMBER, AND E-MAIL ADDRESS>.

First Round Competition Schedule and Locations:

LOCATION	DATE	TIME	PHONE
(Semifinals)*			
(Finals)*			

*The final competition held on <DATE> is open to the public; however, the semifinal competition is not.

All programs are free. To make arrangements for sign-language interpretation, call <PHONE/TDD NUMBERS> at least 48 hours in advance.

Figure 13.7. Library Teen Idol Competition Press Release

Library Teen Idol Competition Press Release

<LIBRARY LOGO>

FOR IMMEDIATE RELEASE
<DATE>

LIBRARY TEEN IDOL COMPETITION

It's not exactly *American Idol*, but it's close! Competition heats up this summer at the <LIBRARY NAME> with a Teen Idol contest. This talent search mimics the popular Fox Television Network show. The library is on a hunt for gifted teens, and one lucky youngster could grab the grand prize, which includes $4,500 worth of studio time. There are also prizes for the 1st and 2nd runner-ups.

There will be three rounds of competition, with the first starting soon at a library branch near you! For directions to a specific library location and for registration information, log onto our Web site at <WEB SITE ADDRESS> or contact <CONTACT NAME, PHONE NUMBER, AND E-MAIL ADDRESS>.

First Round Competition Schedule and Locations:

LOCATION	DATE	TIME	PHONE
(Semifinals)*			
(Finals)*			

*The final competition held on <DATE> is open to the public; however, the semifinal competition is not.

All programs are free. To make arrangements for sign-language interpretation, call <PHONE/TDD NUMBERS> at least 48 hours in advance.

NOTE TO EDITORS: If you need more information for your story, please contact <CONTACT NAME, PHONE NUMBER, AND E-MAIL ADDRESS>.

Figure 13.8. Library Teen Idol Sign-In Sheet

Library Teen Idol Sign-In Sheet

Date: _____

	Name / Song	Phone #	E-mail Address
1.			
2.			
3.			
4.			
5.			
6.			
7.			
8.			
9.			
10.			
11.			
12.			
13.			
14.			
15.			
16.			
17.			
18.			
19.			
20.			

Figure 13.9. Library Teen Idol Performance Roster

Library Teen Idol Performance Roster

Branch: _____

	Contestant	Music / Song
1.		
2.		
3.		
4.		
5.		
6.		
7.		
8.		
9.		
10.		
11.		
12.		
13.		
14.		
15.		
16.		
17.		
18.		
19.		
20.		

Figure 13.10. Library Teen Idol Performance Rating Form

Library Teen Idol Performance Rating Form

Branch: _____

#	Contestant	Music / Song

Rating: 0   1   2   3   4   5

Judge's Comments:

_____
_____
_____
_____
_____
_____

#	Contestant	Music / Song

Rating: 0   1   2   3   4   5

Judge's Comments:

_____
_____
_____
_____
_____
_____

Figure 13.11. Sample Letters to Participants of Semifinals and Grand Finale and to Contest Winners

---

Sample Letters to Participants of the Semifinals and Grand Finale and to Contest Winners

<LIBRARY LOGO>

Dear Teen Idol _____:

CONGRATULATIONS!!! You have been selected to move into our Semifinal competition for Library Teen Idol. We look forward to seeing you on <DATE>, at <LOCATION>.

The judging will begin at <TIME> in the <LOCATION>. You must supply your own music accompaniment. A CD/tape player will be provided. It is also acceptable to sing acapella.

If you have any questions, please don't hesitate to call me at <PHONE NUMBER>.

Good Luck,

<CONTACT NAME>
<ADDRESS>

<LIBRARY LOGO>

Dear Teen Idol _____:

You've made it to the Final Competition for Library Teen Idol. CONGRATULATIONS!!!

The program will begin at <TIME> in the <LOCATION>, <DATE>. You must supply your own musical accompaniment. As usual, a CD/tape player will be provided. It is also acceptable to sing acapella. I suggest that you arrive at least an hour early. That way we can do a "mic check," and you can make sure you have everything ready. You may also get a chance to meet some industry professionals before the show.

Upon arrival, each contestant will draw a number signifying the order in which you will perform. You will wear the number so that you can be identified for the vote. Remember that the audience is the judge this time. It's not just how well you sing, but how you look and your showmanship. So dress the part and act the role. In case of a tie, there will be a "sing off" between those involved, and the audience will vote again.

I wish you the best. We look forward to seeing YOU at the TOP.

If you have any questions, please don't hesitate to call me at <PHONE NUMBER>.

Good Luck,

<CONTACT NAME>
<ADDRESS>

(Cont'd.)

Figure 13.11. Sample Letters to Participants of the Semifinals and Grand Finale and to Contest Winners *(Continued)*

<LIBRARY LOGO>

Dear Teen Idols _____:

CONGRATULATIONS on being winners of our first annual Library Teen Idol contest. The Program was GREAT! And as you know the competition was outstanding. This made the judging very tight and the scores very close. Therefore, in order to recognize the two top contenders, the library will promote both of you, as *American Idol* promoted Rubin and Clay. <NAME>, the Grand Prize Winner, will represent the library at various functions, but we will also promote <NAME>, the 1st place runner-up, by providing opportunities for exposure as well.

The library will be releasing a press release stating this information to the local television stations, newspapers, and radio stations. This will also be posted on the "Teen" page of the library's Web site. Therefore, we need a picture of the two of you. <NAME>, Photographer and Librarian at <LIBRARY NAME>, will contact you to set up a time and place to take the pictures.

Your first performance date, if you are available, will be <DATE>, here at the <LOCATION> at <TIME>. The Teen Advisory Board is hosting <PROGRAM NAME>, which will consist of <PROGRAM DETAILS>. You are asked to perform one number each. Please be responsible for your own musical accompaniment, as usual. A CD/tape player will be provided. I suggest that you arrive at least an hour early. That way we can do a "mic check."

Remember, you will be representing the <LIBRARY NAME> as the Library Teen Idols. Other teens will be looking up to you, so please dress the part and act the role.

Your next performance will be <DATE AND LOCATION>. You will be performing at LibraryFest, the biggest event the library sponsors each year. The purpose of LibraryFest is to enhance the public's awareness of the <LIBRARY NAME>, with emphasis on the collection, programs, services, and facilities, and to generate enthusiasm for reading among the citizens of <CITY/STATE>. Last year there were over <NUMBER> in attendance.

I hope you will be able to participate in both events. If for some reason this causes a conflict with your scheduling, please notify me as soon as possible by return e-mail or by phone.

If you have any questions, please don't hesitate to call me at <PHONE NUMBER>.

I have no doubt; I will see YOU BOTH at the TOP.

Truly,

<CONTACT NAME>
<ADDRESS>

Figure 13.12. Library Teen Idol Ballots for the Final Competition

Figure 13.13. Library Teen Idol Certificate of Recognition

14
POETRY SLAM

PROGRAM DESCRIPTION

A Poetry Slam is the competitive art of performance poetry. Slams have evolved into an international art form emphasizing audience involvement and poetic excellence. The event can be facilitated by a local poetry group or conducted by library staff. A Poetry Slam is a fun way to celebrate National Poetry Month in April with your teens.

PROGRAM GOALS

Slams are more inclusive and cater to a more diverse audience than the typical poetry reading. By making poetry competitive, the slam provides nontraditional audiences an avenue for experiencing poetry in a live setting and at an extremely high performance level. Hosting a Poetry Slam is a way to involve students in writing original poetry and performing their works. This program instills positive values to guide teens (Developmental Assets® #26–31), helps them develop life skills and social competencies (Developmental Assets #32–36), and nurtures, celebrates, and affirms their positive identity (Developmental Assets #37–40).

HOW TO DO IT

Step 1: Make a Plan

Ask a local poetry or writers group to host the Poetry Slam, or you can host it yourself. Library personnel and Teen Advisory Board members can help staff the event.

Slam poets have three minutes and ten seconds to perform their original poetry without props. There is a one-half point deduction for each ten seconds over the three minutes and ten seconds. Five judges are picked randomly from the audience. The judges have two sets of score cards, one set numbered from 0 to 10 (whole number cards are held in the right hand) and one set numbered from .1 to .9 (the decimal cards are held in the left hand). Judges score each slam poet on content, performance, and style. A scorekeeper tosses out the high and the low scores for each poet and adds the remaining three scores for a total score for the round.

Half of the poets, the ones with the highest scores, proceed to a second round. New judges are selected from the audience. The poets read another poem, are judged as in the first round, and the half of the poets with the highest scores proceed to the third and final round. Once again these poets perform a third original poem, and their scores determine their placement. The highest score wins the slam. Alternatively, if you want to complete the competition in two rounds, the scores from round one and two are added together to determine the winner. Prizes are awarded for first, second, and third places. To award prize money of, for example, $90.00, award $50 for first place, $25 for second place, and $15 for third place.

Step 2: Set a Date, Book a Space

April is National Poetry Month and a perfect time to host a Poetry Slam for teens. About one and a half hours is long enough for the competition and awards.

A small stage area for the poet and seating for the audience are the basic needs. If you have the space, a café setting with small tables and coffeehouse refreshments add to the atmosphere.

Step 3: Book the Presenter

Teens provide the entertainment with their poetry performances in this program. The librarian or a writing group member emcees the event. Audience members are chosen to be the judges.

Step 4: Create a Program Format and Agenda

- Round one: All poets read an original poem, and each poet is judged immediately after performing. Half of the poets with the highest scores proceed to round two. The emcee announces who will proceed.
- Round two: New judges are selected. The top scoring poets read a second original poem, and each is judged immediately after performing. Once again half the poets proceed to round three, announced by the emcee.
- Round three: In the last round, the highest-scoring poets now read for placement. New judges score after each reading. The highest score wins first, second highest wins second, and third highest wins third place.
- Award the prizes.

Step 5: Market the Program

Create flyers and rave cards (see Figures 14.1 and 14.2) to advertise the event, and distribute them to schools, Boys & Girls Clubs, and homeschooler and other local youth organizations. Post flyers at teen hot spots and centers.

Step 6: Gather Materials

Make five sets of score cards for the judges. Number them as follows: 1, 2, 3, 4, 5, 6, 7, 8, 9, 10 for the right-hand set and .0, .1, .2, .3, .4, .5, .6, .7, .8, .9 for the left-hand set. Make a score sheet for the scorekeeper, with one column for poets' names, five columns for the judges' scores, and a final column for the total score for the poet for each round.

Place gift cards or cash prizes in envelopes and mark first, second, and third places. Prepare refreshments if serving any. Writing journals and pens are nice for participation prizes if you have an inexpensive resource for them. Assemble books for a display during the program.

Book List

Alderson, Daniel. 1996. *Talking Back to Poems: A Working Guide for the Aspiring Poet.* Berkeley, CA: Celestial Arts.

Figure 14.1. Poetry Slam Publicity Flyer

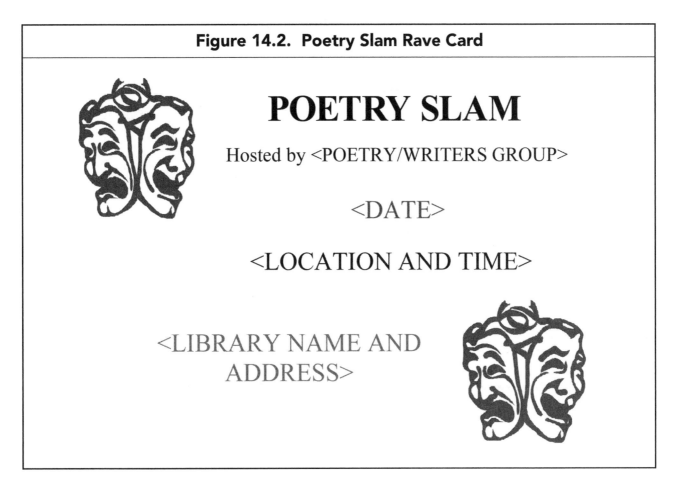

Figure 14.2. Poetry Slam Rave Card

POETRY SLAM

Hosted by <POETRY/WRITERS GROUP>

<DATE>

<LOCATION AND TIME>

<LIBRARY NAME AND ADDRESS>

Burkhardt, Ross M. 2006. *Using Poetry in the Classroom: Engaging Students in Learning.* Lanham, MD: Rowman & Littlefield Education.

Day, Lucille and Doug Dworkin, illus. 2005. *Chain Letter*. Berkeley, CA: Heyday Books.

Fletcher, Ralph J. 2002. *Poetry Matters: Writing a Poem from the Inside Out*. New York: HarperTrophy.

Hewitt, Geof. 1998. *Today You Are My Favorite Poet: Writing Poems with Teenagers.* Portsmouth, NH: Heinemann.

Livingston, Myra Cohn. 1991. *Poem-making: Ways to Begin Writing Poetry*. New York: HarperCollins.

Mock, Jeff. 1998. *You Can Write Poetry*. Cincinnati: Writer's Digest Books.

Weiss, Jen and Scott Herndon. 2001. *Brave New Voices: The Youth Speaks Guide to Teaching Spoken-Word Poetry*. Portsmouth, NH: Heinemann.

Wong, Janet S. and Theresa Flavin, illus. 2002. *You Have to Write*. New York: Margaret K. McElderry Books.

Step 7: Set Up the Program Area

Set up the meeting room or auditorium audience style with a staging area for the poet. You can dress up the performance area with a black curtain background and a stool for the poet to sit on. In a large room, a microphone would be helpful. If you want to create a coffee-house setting, use small tables (card tables will do).

Step 8: Conduct the Event

Select a scorekeeper from the audience or the writers group or a Teen Advisory Board member to record scores. Select five judges randomly from the audience, and give them the score cards. Explain to them how they will judge by rating the poets with the score cards based on the poets' performances. Invite the audience to applaud the poets but freely cheer or boo the judges to show if they agree or disagree with their scoring. Follow the planned agenda for conducting the rounds of competition.

Step 9: Evaluate the Program

Evaluations are helpful for planning future programs. Customize the evaluation form from Part I (see Figure I.3 on CD) for participants to fill out. Collect the forms as the audience leaves.

15
TEEN ADVISORY BOARD

PROGRAM DESCRIPTION

A Teen Advisory Board (TAB) gives teens a sense of ownership and responsibility in their library. Having a specific area designated as a teen center, if possible, also provides an opportunity for TABs to shape the direction of teen services by suggesting collections and resources of interest to them. They can also host all teen social activities and events. The TAB meets regularly once or twice a month, and the teens lead the meetings. Refreshments are always on hand.

PROGRAM GOALS

The goal is to improve youth services by increasing teen involvement. A Teen Advisory Board supports teens with love, care, and attention (Developmental Assets® #1–6), empowers them with opportunities to make a difference in their family and community (Developmental Assets #7–10), establishes clear boundaries and has high expectations (Developmental Assets #11–16), helps teens find activities that make constructive use of their time (Developmental Assets #17–20), nurtures in them a commitment to learning (Developmental Assets #21–25), instills positive values to guide them (Developmental Assets #26–31), helps them develop life skills and social competencies (Developmental Assets #32–36), and nurtures, celebrates, and affirms their positive identity (Developmental Assets #37–40).

HOW TO DO IT

Step 1: Make a Plan

To find teens to participate, take a poll or put out questionnaires with a collection box asking teens to sign up if they are interested in becoming a voice in the library, helping plan programs, and making other library decisions that affect teens. Set up meeting times that fit with interested teens' schedules.

Step 2: Set a Date, Book a Space

TABs can meet once or twice a month and even more frequently when working on a project. Most groups can accomplish what they need to do in a one to one and a half hour meeting. Establish a regular meeting time each month. Our experience is two meetings a month work best, but one may work better for your teens. Instead of saying "every other week" (which can be confusing for teens), it is better to say "every first and third" or "every second and fourth" (your selected day of the week). A meeting room (if no teen center is available) where teens can talk and eat and work on projects is the ideal space for the TAB to meet.

Step 3: Book the Presenter

Presenters are not necessary for TAB meetings, but library staff members can be invited to talk about their jobs in the library a few times a year to inspire future librarians. Other guests can also be invited to speak.

Step 4: Create a Program Format and Agenda

A printed agenda for each TAB member is helpful to keep the meeting on track, and it also gives them somewhere to write notes. Topics might include collection development, future programs, and volunteer opportunities and any issues or concerns involving teens at the library. Review the agenda with the teen meeting leader before the meeting to clarify any questions. Most advisors prefer to stay in the room to supervise and also make note of any great ideas and add important information as ideas are being generated.

Step 5: Market the Program

Create rave cards (see Figure 15.1) to advertise the board and distribute to the schools, home-schooler organizations, and the teen area of the library. Send out a press release inviting teens to join, and create applications for those looking to join (see Figure 15.2). TAB members can distribute rave cards to friends to recruit new members and invite guests to meetings.

Step 6: Gather Materials

Prepare an agenda of items the teens need to discuss. Prepare refreshments for the teens.

Book List

Alessio, Amy J. and Kimberly A. Patton. 2007. *A Year of Programs for Teens*. Chicago: American Library Association.

Anderson, Sheila B. 2007. *Serving Young Teens and 'Tweens*. Westport, CT: Libraries Unlimited.

Burek Pierce, Jennifer. 2008. *Sex, Brains, and Video Games: A Librarian's Guide to Teens in the Twenty-first Century*. Chicago: American Library Association.

Edwards, Kirsten. 2002. *Teen Library Events: A Month-by-Month Guide*. Westport, CT: Greenwood Press.

Graham, Stedman. 2000. *Teens Can Make It Happen: Nine Steps to Success*. New York: Simon & Schuster.

Honnold, RoseMary. 2002. *101+ Teen Programs That Work*. New York: Neal-Schuman.

Honnold, RoseMary. 2005. *More Teen Programs That Work*. New York: Neal-Schuman.

Jones, Patrick and Joel Shoemaker. 2001. *Do It Right! Best Practices for Serving Young Adults in School and Public Libraries*. New York: Neal-Schuman.

Mondowney, JoAnn G. 2001. *Hold Them in Your Heart: Successful Strategies for Library Services to At-Risk Teens*. New York: Neal-Schuman.

Ott, Valerie A. 2006. *Teen Programs with Punch: A Month-by-Month Guide*. Westport, CT: Libraries Unlimited.

Peterson, Jean Sunde. 2007. *The Essential Guide to Talking with Teens: Ready-to-Use Discussions for School and Youth Groups*. Minneapolis: Free Spirit.

Teens' Guide to College & Career Planning: Your High School Roadmap for College & Career Success. 2008. Lawrenceville, NJ: Peterson's.

Figure 15.1. Teen Advisory Board Rave Card

Figure 15.2. Application to Join the Teen Advisory Board

Application to Join the Teen Advisory Board

<LIBRARY LOGO>

**NEW MEMBERS
TEEN ADVISORY BOARD**

Name: _____

      (Last)   (First)   (Middle)

Address: _____

_____

_____

Home Phone Number: _____

E-mail Address: _____

Library Branch: _____

What do you like most about coming to the library?

What would you like to see added to <TEEN CENTER>?

Hobbies:

Texas State Library and Archives Commission. 2000. *Public Library Advisory Board Handbook*. Austin: Library Development Division, Texas State Library and Archives Commission.

Step 7: Set Up the Program Area

TAB meetings can take place in the teen area, a meeting room, or even in a fast food restaurant. Space to sit and a place for refreshments are all you need, but tables are necessary if the teens are working on a project during the meeting. The meeting must be in a space where teens can talk freely without disturbing staff or library patrons.

Step 8: Conduct the Event

Each TAB meeting will be different, depending on what the teens need to work on. A written agenda will keep them on track, and a teen should record any decisions and suggestions they make.

Step 9: Evaluate the Program

Evaluations are helpful for planning future programs. Customize the evaluation form from Part I (see Figure I.3 on CD) for participants to fill out. Collect the forms as the audience leaves.

16
YOUTH LEADERSHIP CONFERENCE

PROGRAM DESCRIPTION

The Youth Leadership Conference is an interactive conference featuring city leaders who encourage youth to acquire the leadership skills necessary for them to make meaningful contributions to the community.

PROGRAM GOALS

Participants have opportunities to learn from city leaders, public officials, and other young leaders. The program is designed to inspire today's youth to reach their full leadership potential and to identify ways to improve policies and support for young people. If we strengthen our young people today, we will be sure to have sound, effective leaders tomorrow. People 18 years of age and younger make up only 25 percent of our population today, but they are 100 percent of our future. This program supports teens with love, care, and attention (Developmental Assets® #1–6), empowers them with opportunities to make a difference in their family and community (Developmental Assets #7–10), establishes clear boundaries and has high expectations (Developmental Assets #11–16), nurtures in teens a commitment to learning (Developmental Assets #21–25), instills positive values to guide them (Developmental Assets #26–31), helps teens develop life skills and social competencies (Developmental Assets #32–36), and nurtures, celebrates, and affirms their positive identity (Developmental Assets #37–40).

HOW TO DO IT

Step 1: Make a Plan

Ask your city's mayor to proclaim the program day "Citywide Youth Day," with the proclamation presented to the Teen Advisory Board (TAB). Plan to provide lunch to the participants, and ask a poetry group to perform during lunch. Ask a local community leader or a local radio or TV personality and a representative from the TAB to moderate an interactive panel discussion in which young people from the audience ask questions and get answers. The guest speakers will make up the panel. Invite a local musical group to perform at the conference. Request a grant to pay for lunch, or ask local restaurants for donated boxed lunches.

Step 2: Set a Date, Book a Space

Schedule the event in the summer when school is out. It is an all-day event, so a Saturday works well.

Book a lecture hall, auditorium, or large meeting room for the program. If your library doesn't have such a facility, consider a nearby school auditorium, the Boys & Girls Club, a recreation center, a community room, or a church meeting room.

Step 3: Book the Presenter

Contact motivational speakers, such as city leaders, city council members, business leaders, and youth leaders, by telephone to participate in a one-day seminar that will consist of a panel discussion along with a few break-out workshop sessions. Follow up with a letter that tells the details of the event. Invite a local recording artist or music group to perform at the beginning, middle, and end of the conference.

Suggested topics for speakers and for discussions include the following: a leader knows where he is going and can inspire others to go with him; leadership is first being, then doing; a good leader is one who leads others to leadership; effectiveness is not doing things right, but doing the right things; the greatest display of leadership is service (Munroe, 1999).

Step 4: Create a Program Format and Agenda

Time	Activity	Presenter
10:00	Doors open	Music group
10:30	Welcome and introduction of Teen Advisory Board	Librarian; Mistress of Ceremonies: a Teen Advisory Board member
10:45	Inspirational words	Minister
10:50	Song	Music group
10:55	Speaker #1	Doctor
11:10	Speaker #2	Teen Advisory Board PR
	Speaker #3	Teen Advisory Board President
11:25	Performance	Music group
11:30	Speaker #4	Judge
11:45	Speaker #5	Minister
12:00	Lunch and performance	Poetry group
1:00	Speaker #6	Youth director
1:15	Speaker #7	Attorney
1:30	Performance	Music group
1:45	Speaker #8	Councilman
2:00	Speaker #9	Councilwoman
2:15	Speaker #10	Mayor
2:30	Panel discussion	Moderator
4:00	Performance	Music group
5:00	Closing remarks	

Step 5: Market the Program

Send out a press release (see Figure 16.1). Create rave cards and flyers (see Figures 16.2 and 16.3) to advertise the event. Contact various organizations such as the Boys & Girls Clubs, and post flyers at various teen hot spots and centers.

Figure 16.1. Youth Leadership Conference Press Release

Youth Leadership Conference Press Release

<LIBRARY LOGO>

NEWS RELEASE
<DATE>
FOR IMMEDIATE RELEASE
<CONTACT>

YOUTH LEADERSHIP CONFERENCE
"Leaders of Today Preparing Youth Leaders for Tomorrow"

(<CITY/STATE>) Though it may be true that people 18 years of age and younger make up only 25 percent of our population, they are 100 percent of our future. With this in mind, the <LIBRARY NAME> Teen Advisory Board is sponsoring a citywide Youth Leadership Conference, to be held <DATE, TIME FRAME, AND LOCATION>. Doors will open at <TIME> with music by <BAND NAME>.

This day has been proclaimed "Citywide Youth Day" by the Mayor's Office. A proclamation will be presented to the Board. The conference goals are to help prepare the next generation of leaders and to identify ways to improve policies and support for young people.

<PARTICIPATING ORGANIZATIONS' NAMES> will host the youth leadership conference. Their mission is to increase opportunities for young people to build successful lives and to educate them on how to become great leaders in the community. The purpose of the conference is to instruct, enrich, and enthuse promising young people, preparing them for a lifetime of leadership with an unforgettable experience. Participants will have exciting opportunities to learn from city leaders, public officials, and other young leaders from all over the city.

Designed to inspire today's youth to reach their full leadership potential, the program will feature guest speakers such as <PARTICIPATING INDIVIDUALS' NAMES>. The speakers will encourage youth to obtain the leadership skills necessary for them to make meaningful contributions to our community and to embark on a lifelong journey of leadership and service.

This youth leadership conference will address the meaning of service and the importance of young people's contributions to their community through service by focusing on the meaning of service to the individual, the community, and the nation and providing a framework of how young people can put their leadership skills into action. The conference will be filled with fun, food, and entertainment.

Lunch will be provided, during which <PERFORMANCE ARTISTS' NAMES> will perform live poetry. After lunch <MODERATOR'S NAME> will moderate an interactive panel discussion in which young people from the audience will ask questions and get answers. The guest speakers will make up the panel, providing varying perspectives on the social needs and issues of the community. The conference will conclude with a performance by <BAND NAME>.

If you are interested in the future of our city, come participate in this educational experience of a lifetime.

- SHARE IDEAS for improving the lives of young people.
- NETWORK with past and future leaders, and make contacts that will spark new ideas and inspire you to work toward your dreams.

To make arrangements for sign-language interpretation, call <PHONE/TDD NUMBERS> at least 48 hours in advance.

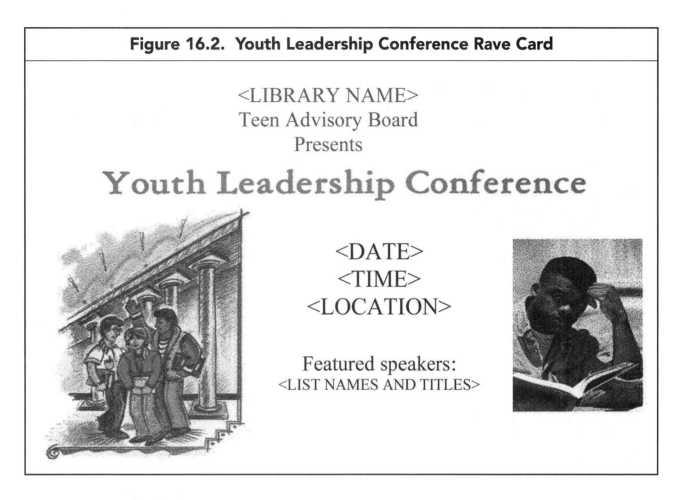

Figure 16.2. Youth Leadership Conference Rave Card

<LIBRARY NAME>
Teen Advisory Board
Presents

Youth Leadership Conference

<DATE>
<TIME>
<LOCATION>

Featured speakers:
<LIST NAMES AND TITLES>

Step 6: Gather Materials

Assemble books for a display during the program.

Book List

Bachel, Beverly K. 2001. *What Do You Really Want? How to Set a Goal and Go for It! A Guide for Teens*. Minneapolis: Free Spirit.

Carney, Mary Lou. 2002. *The Power of Positive Thinking for Teens*. Nashville: Ideals Publications.

Cherniss, Hilary and Sara Jane Sluke. 2002. *The Complete Idiot's Guide to Peer Pressure for Teens*. Indianapolis: Alpha.

Desetta, Al and Educators for Social Responsibility. 2005. *The Courage to Be Yourself: True Stories by Teens About Cliques, Conflicts, and Overcoming Peer Pressure*. Minneapolis: Free Spirit.

Friel, John C. and Linda D. Friel. 2000. *The 7 Best Things (Smart) Teens Do*. Deerfield Beach, FL: Health Communications.

Johnson, Robert L. and Paulette Stanford. 2002. *Strength for Their Journey: Five Essential Disciplines African American Parents Must Teach Their Children and Teens*. New York: Harlem Moon/Broadway Books.

Johnson, Spencer. 2002. *Who Moved My Cheese? For Teens*. New York: G.P. Putnam's Sons.

Figure 16.3. Youth Leadership Conference Publicity Flyer

Youth Leadership Conference

Hosted by

<PARTICIPATING ORGANIZATIONS' NAMES>

Guest Speakers and Discussion Panel

<DATE>
<TIME>
<LOCATION>

There will be food, fun and entertainment

Sponsored by

The <LIBRARY NAME>
Teen Advisory Board

Leslie, Roger. 2004. *Success Express for Teens: 50 Activities That Will Change Your Life*. Houston: Bayou.

Lewis, Barbara A. and Pamela Espeland. 2005. *What Do You Stand For? For Teens: A Guide to Building Character*. Minneapolis: Free Spirit.

McGraw, Jay. 2000. *Life Strategies for Teens*. New York: Simon & Schuster Audio.

Munroe, Myles. 1999. *Myles Munroe on Leadership*. Lanham, MD: Pneuma Life Publishing.

Zielin, Lara. 2003. *Make Things Happen: The Key to Networking for Teens*. Montreal: Lobster Press.

Step 7: Set Up the Program Area

Set up the auditorium for the conference with a podium for the moderator and tables and chairs for the panel, with microphones for the moderator and panelists. Prepare a place for lunch.

Step 8: Conduct the Event

Follow the prepared agenda.

Step 9: Evaluate the Program

Evaluations are helpful for planning future programs. Customize the evaluation form from Part I (see Figure I.3 on CD) for participants to fill out. Collect the forms as the audience leaves.

Chapter 4

OUTSIDE THE LIBRARY: PROGRAMS TO GO

17
COMMITMENT TO FITNESS

PROGRAM DESCRIPTION

Promote physical fitness through jump rope sessions once a week at the library. Jumping rope is one of the most efficient methods of cardiovascular training and an excellent way to burn calories. You can jump rope virtually anywhere, and it costs almost nothing for quality equipment. Best of all, it's easy to learn!

PROGRAM GOALS

The Commitment to Fitness program inspires, motivates, and educates teens and adults to have fun while exercising. The whole family can participate in a healthy activity in the library that promotes awareness of the library's resources and promotes the library as a community center. This program supports teens with love, care, and attention (Developmental Assets® #1–6), helps teens find activities that make constructive use of their time (Developmental Assets #17–20), instills positive values to guide them (Developmental Assets #26–31), helps them develop life skills and social competencies (Developmental Assets #32–36), and nurtures, celebrates, and affirms their positive identity (Developmental Assets #37–40).

HOW TO DO IT

Step 1: Make a Plan

According to a national survey conducted for the Calorie Control Council, 58 percent of Americans admit they need to lose weight and 37 percent acknowledge they need to lose ten pounds or more. Some of these people live in your community. Suggest that the participants see a physician before beginning to jump rope or any exercise program. Even if they are in good shape, they should start slow by gradually increasing session times over two to three weeks to let the leg muscles get accustomed to the extra exercise.

Request a grant to pay for jump ropes, but encourage participants to provide their own. This would show a commitment to the program, and participants can keep the ropes to continue the exercise program at home. Those completing 12 weeks of jumping rope three to five times a week will receive a certificate of completion.

Step 2: Set a Date, Book a Space

Start the program the first week after New Year's Day in January when patrons are ready to make a new commitment to an exercise program. Continue the sessions for 12 weeks, ending the last week in March. Hold sessions one to three days a week for 20 to 30 minutes a day. Like all forms of cardiovascular training, aerobic movement must be performed three to five times per week for at least 12 weeks for the benefits of training to become apparent. Just ten minutes of jumping rope is equivalent to a one-mile run. If one session is held at the library, encourage jumpers to complete two more sessions each week at home with family or friends.

Use an area for the jump rope program where the floor surface is even, nonabrasive, and limits friction. Look for a cushioned surface, but not carpet, to jump on. A concrete floor is hard on the knees.

Step 3: Book the Presenter

No presenter is necessary for this program.

Step 4: Create a Program Format and Agenda

The sessions do not consist of jumping rope continuously. There should be rest breaks as well as time to talk about the many resources available in the library.

Stretches	Easy listening music	Light stretching exercises
Warm up	Moderate tempo music	Slowly jump rope or walk in place
Workout	Upbeat music	Jump rope in time with the music
Cool down	Slow soothing music	Slowly jump rope or walk in place

Step 5: Market the Program

Create rave cards and flyers (see Figures 17.1 and 17.2) to advertise the program, and distribute them to various places, including walking parks. Send out a press release. Contact various organizations such as the Boys & Girls Clubs, senior citizens organizations, and the YWCA. Distribute rave cards to local businesses and restaurants. Post flyers in the library, at daycare centers, and at apartment complexes.

Step 6: Gather Materials

A video that may help you prepare called *Ready, Set, Jump!* is available from the American Heart Association. You need a CD player and a selection of upbeat music CDs. The sessions consist of about four songs. The first one should be easy listening music to warm up. The next two should be upbeat. Ten minutes of fast rope skipping gives a person a brief aerobic workout. The last song should be a smooth jazz type to cool down. Books of songs and poems for participants to memorize and recite while jumping rope will add variety.

Participants should wear well-cushioned footwear and comfortable loose-fitting clothing. Everyone can bring their own ropes. When selecting a rope, step on the middle of the rope. The end sections of the rope should fit comfortably in your hands and reach the middle of your chest.

Assemble a display of books on health and exercise. Create a rules and information sheet (see Figure 17.3) to give each participant and certificates (see Figure 17.4) to give to those who complete the course.

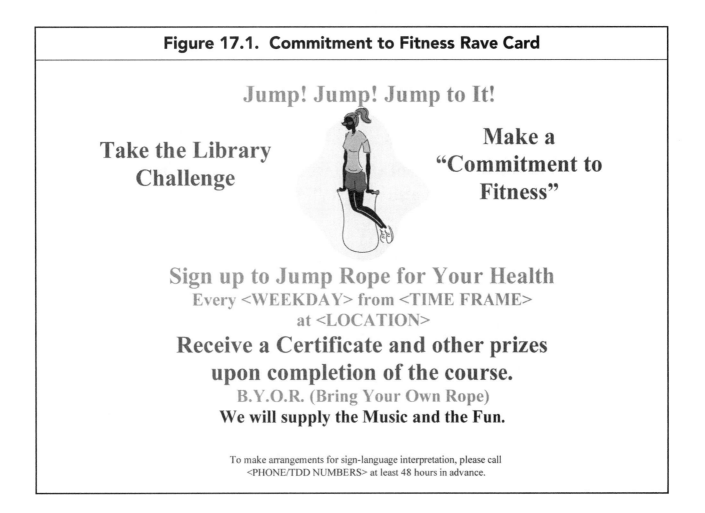

Figure 17.1. Commitment to Fitness Rave Card

Jump! Jump! Jump to It!

Take the Library Challenge

Make a "Commitment to Fitness"

Sign up to Jump Rope for Your Health
Every <WEEKDAY> from <TIME FRAME>
at <LOCATION>
**Receive a Certificate and other prizes
upon completion of the course.**
B.Y.O.R. (Bring Your Own Rope)
We will supply the Music and the Fun.

To make arrangements for sign-language interpretation, please call
<PHONE/TDD NUMBERS> at least 48 hours in advance.

Book List

Belliner, Karen. 2004. *Fitness Information for Teens: Health Tips About Exercise, Physical Well-being, and Health Maintenance.* Detroit: Omnigraphics.

Boardman, Bob. 1993. *Red Hot Peppers: The Skookum Book of Jump Rope Games, Rhymes, and Fancy Footwork.* Seattle: Sasquatch Books.

Ellerbusch, Kristin. 1992. *Jump-rope Rap.* Chicago: The Child's World.

Fletcher, Anne M. 2006. *Weight Loss Confidential: How Teens Lose Weight and Keep It Off—And What They Wish Parents Knew.* Boston: Houghton Mifflin.

Lawton, Sandra Augustyn. 2007. *Body Information for Teens: Health Tips About Maintaining Well-being for a Lifetime.* Detroit: Omnigraphics.

Lee, Buddy. 2003. *Jump Rope Training: Techniques and Programs for Improved Fitness and Performance.* Champaign, IL: Human Kinetics.

McGraw, Jay. 2003. *The Ultimate Weight Solution for Teens: The 7 Keys to Weight Freedom.* New York: Free Press.

Sammons, Mary Beth, Samantha Moss, and Azadeh Houshyar, illus. 2005. *InSPAration: A Teen's Guide to Healthy Living Inspired by Today's Top Spas.* New York: Watson-Guptill.

Schlosberg, Suzanne and Liz Neporent. 2005. *Fitness for Dummies.* Weinheim, Germany: Wiley-VCH.

Winkler, Martin. 2007. *RopeSport: The Ultimate Jump Rope Workout.* New York: Wiley.

Figure 17.2. Commitment to Fitness Publicity Flyer

Jump! Jump! Jump to It!

Jumping rope is one of the most efficient methods of cardiovascular training and an excellent way to burn calories.

Take the Library Challenge

Make a "Commitment to Fitness"

Sign up to Jump Rope for Your Health
Every <WEEKDAY> from <TIME FRAME>
at <LOCATION>

Receive a Certificate and other prizes upon completion of the course.

B.Y.O.R. (Bring Your Own Rope)

We will supply the Music and the Fun.

<LIBRARY LOGO>

To make arrangements for sign-language interpretation, call
<PHONE/TDD NUMBERS> at least 48 hours in advance.

Figure 17.3. Commitment to Fitness Rules

Commitment to Fitness Rules

Name: _____   Date Started: _____

Simple Techniques:

- Your body should be erect but relaxed when you jump.
- You should look straight ahead, not at your feet.
- Land on the balls of your feet, not on your heels.
- Keep your knees slightly bent.
- Try not to move your arms much.

Provide your own jump rope.
Choose well-cushioned footwear and comfortable, loose-fitting clothing.

Like all forms of cardiovascular training, aerobic movement must be performed 3 to 5 times per week for at least 12 weeks for the benefits of training to become apparent. At the finish, turn your log sheet in at your library. Those completing 12 weeks of jumping rope 3 to 5 times a week will receive a certificate of completion.

Please see a physician before beginning to jump rope or starting any other exercise program.

Commitment to Fitness
Daily Log Sheet

Put an X in the box for each day that you jump rope for the next twelve weeks, whether you jump at the library or at home. Total each week in the space provided. The goal is to jump 3 to 5 days a week for 12 consecutive weeks. Make a Commitment to Fitness.

Day	Week 1	Week 2	Week 3	Week 4	Week 5	Week 6	Week 7	Week 8	Week 9	Week 10	Week 11	Week 12
Sun												
Mon												
Tues												
Wed												
Thurs												
Fri												
Sat												
Sun												
Total												

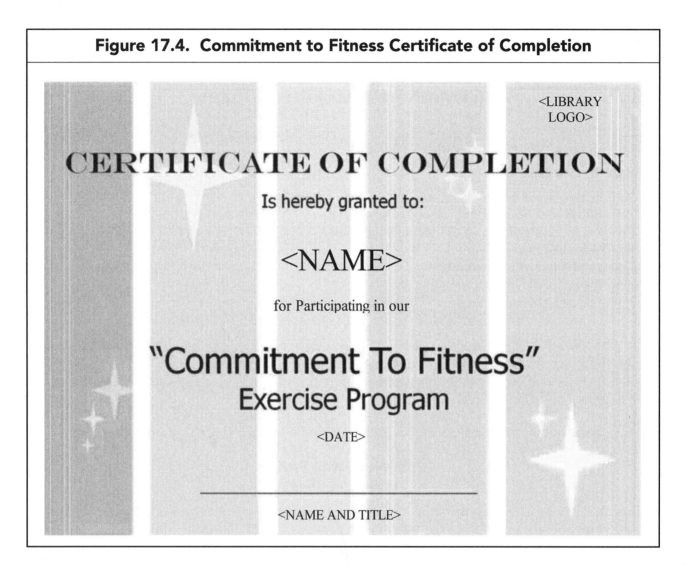

Figure 17.4. Commitment to Fitness Certificate of Completion

Yolen, Jane. 1992. *Street Rhymes Around the World*. Honesdale, PA: Wordsong.
Youngs, Jennifer Leigh. 2000. *Feeling Great, Looking Hot, & Loving Yourself! Health, Fitness & Beauty for Teens*. Deerfield Beach, FL: Health Communications.

Step 7: Set Up the Program Area

Set up a room for the exercise session. Jumpers need plenty of room. Set up the CD player and CDs. Display books on health and exercise.

Step 8: Conduct the Event

Follow the planned agenda, varying the music at each session.

Step 9: Evaluate the Program

Evaluations are helpful for planning future programs. Customize the evaluation form from Part I (see Figure I.3 on CD) for participants to fill out. Collect the forms as the audience leaves.

18
C.L.A.S.S.: CONNECTING LIBRARIES AND SCHOOLS SIMULTANEOUSLY

PROGRAM DESCRIPTION

Connecting Libraries and Schools Simultaneously (C.L.A.S.S.) is a year-long library card sign-up campaign that is a collaborative partnership between the schools and the library to support reading and learning at school and in the home.

A library card sign-up campaign is a way to remind parents, teachers, and youth that a library card is the most important school supply of all. The campaign promotes not only library card sign-up but also other library services: class tours and visits, teacher in-service training workshops, and summer reading book lists and library activities. Make teachers aware of the many resources available to them at the public library. Begin by simply adding a library card to the school supply lists.

PROGRAM GOALS

The C.L.A.S.S. library card campaign supports collaboration and cooperation between the schools and the libraries, encourages family reading and family literacy, and increases community awareness and use of public libraries. A library card allows students to borrow books and other materials, access online databases, and renew or reserve books from home. This program supports teens with love, care, and attention (Developmental Assets® #1–6), empowers them with opportunities to make a difference in their family and community (Developmental Assets #7–10), establishes clear boundaries and has high expectations (Developmental Assets #11–16), and nurtures in them a commitment to learning (Developmental Assets #21–25).

HOW TO DO IT

Step 1: Make a Plan

This year-long collaboration will bring the school and public libraries closer together as the librarians work to promote reading and show teachers all the resources available to them. Discuss it with the local school district administrators, and schedule meetings with the curriculum directors and English Language Arts. The PowerPoint Presentation to Promote C.L.A.S.S. on the accompanying CD (and shown in Figure 18.1) is a useful way to help explain your ideas and can be customized for your library. Request funds to pay for advertisements and sign-up incentives.

Figure 18.1. PowerPoint Presentation to Promote C.L.A.S.S.

C.L.A.S.S.
Connecting Libraries And Schools Simultaneously

Library Card Sign-Up Campaign

Presented by <NAME>
<AFFILIATION>
<E-MAIL ADDRESS>

GOALS

✓ 1. To support collaboration and cooperation between <CITY/STATE> public libraries and schools.

✓ 2. To encourage family reading and family literacy and make it enjoyable.

✓ 3. To increase community awareness and use of public libraries.

I. SITUATION

Reading is the fundamental building block of learning in our society.

A child who cannot read is at a serious disadvantage.

Despite the efforts and concerns of educators, acquiring basic literacy skills remains the single most critical problem among schoolchildren.

The SITUATION Continues…

Our schools cannot bear the full burden for developing reading skills in young people.

Meeting this challenge requires the cooperation of parents, caregivers, teachers, community groups . . . *and libraries.*

II. MY IDEA

Allow <LIBRARY NAME> to help you bear the burden of developing reading skills in our youth by working together to organize a library card sign-up campaign:

C.L.A.S.S.

"Connecting Libraries And Schools Simultaneously "

The CARD

<IMAGE OF LIBRARY CARD>

A library card allows students to do more than simply borrow books and other materials.

They can also use their card to access online databases and renew or reserve books from home.

(Cont'd.)

Figure 18.1. PowerPoint Presentation to Promote C.L.A.S.S. *(Continued)*

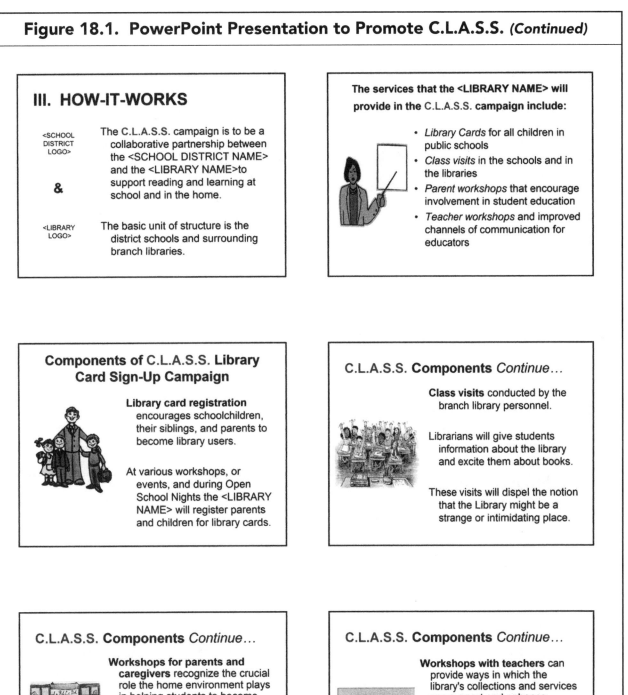

III. HOW-IT-WORKS

<SCHOOL DISTRICT LOGO>

&

<LIBRARY LOGO>

The C.L.A.S.S. campaign is to be a collaborative partnership between the <SCHOOL DISTRICT NAME> and the <LIBRARY NAME> to support reading and learning at school and in the home.

The basic unit of structure is the district schools and surrounding branch libraries.

The services that the <LIBRARY NAME> will provide in the C.L.A.S.S. campaign include:

- *Library Cards* for all children in public schools
- *Class visits* in the schools and in the libraries
- *Parent workshops* that encourage involvement in student education
- *Teacher workshops* and improved channels of communication for educators

---

Components of C.L.A.S.S. Library Card Sign-Up Campaign

Library card registration encourages schoolchildren, their siblings, and parents to become library users.

At various workshops, or events, and during Open School Nights the <LIBRARY NAME> will register parents and children for library cards.

C.L.A.S.S. Components *Continue...*

Class visits conducted by the branch library personnel.

Librarians will give students information about the library and excite them about books.

These visits will dispel the notion that the Library might be a strange or intimidating place.

C.L.A.S.S. Components *Continue...*

Workshops for parents and caregivers recognize the crucial role the home environment plays in helping students to become better readers.

<LIBRARY NAME> can offer tips on reading aloud, how to select books for various age levels, and play activities which can help develop reading skills.

C.L.A.S.S. Components *Continue...*

Workshops with teachers can provide ways in which the library's collections and services can support and enhance classroom activities.

With Assignment Alert forms, teachers can give branch librarians advance notice of class projects so that appropriate materials can be on hand for student use in the libraries.

(Cont'd.)

Figure 18.1. PowerPoint Presentation to Promote C.L.A.S.S. *(Continued)*

C.L.A.S.S. **Components** *Continue…*

Programs for school librarians can keep the public library staff in contact with their professional colleagues at the school.

<LIBRARY NAME> is not a replacement for on-site school libraries.

In fact, experience has shown that public libraries are most successful in communities with a strong school library program.

IV. BENEFITS

The C.L.A.S.S. campaign is designed to make reading and books an integral part of the lives of schoolchildren.

Through a series of programs it will create new links among teachers, school and public librarians, and parents to encourage children to read and make the fullest possible use of their neighborhood libraries.

BENEFITS *Continue…*

The C.L.A.S.S. campaign's greatest strength is that it makes partners of our public schools and branch libraries.

Working together we can provide coordinated programs and activities to bring students and books together, that will focus on family reading and foster a literate community environment.

V. EASY NEXT STEP

The C.L.A.S.S. campaign can dramatically alter the way public libraries work with schools.

Through this campaign the <LIBRARY NAME> will be able to assist the <SCHOOL DISTRICT NAME> in providing tools for learning, understanding, enjoyment, and hope for the future of all students.

The **Close**

The Easy-Next-Step is the approval and implementation of this library card sign up campaign:
C.L.A.S.S.
Connecting Libraries And School Simultaneously

Let's set a date to continue working together to develop activities that will further our common goals once a month, or would every other month be better?

For more information contact:

<NAME>
<TITLE>
<AFFILIATION>
<LIBRARY NAME>
<PHONE NUMBER>
<E-MAIL ADDRESS>

<LIBRARY LOGO>

Step 2: Set a Date, Book a Space

For a year-long campaign, begin in September during National Library Card Sign-Up Month and continue through to the end of the following Summer Reading Program. The campaign takes place in the community school districts and surrounding branch libraries. Campaigns can be held over lunch periods, in English classes, or during school library periods.

Step 3: Book the Presenter

Libraries make any required presentations and tours with classes and teachers.

Step 4: Create a Program Format and Agenda

The services that the library provides in this campaign include the following:

- *Library cards* for all students in public schools, encouraging schoolchildren, their siblings, and parents to become library users
- *Class tours and visits* conducted by library personnel, giving students information about the library and exciting them about books
- *Teacher in-service training workshops*, showing ways in which the library's collections and services support and enhance classroom activities (see Program #25 for an example)
- *Summer reading* book lists and library activities, providing some structure when students are out of school

Step 5: Market the Program

Create flyers/rave cards (see Figure 18.2) and bookmarks (see Figure 18.3) to advertise the events, and distribute them to the schools and branch libraries. Keep schools informed of library programs. Communicate with schools to ensure libraries are in tune with the curricula and assignments.

Step 6: Gather Materials, Prepare Handouts

Library applications and library cards are needed. Include any new patron information your library gives to new users. Prepare handouts of the PowerPoint presentation to give to educators.

Book List

Farmer, Lesley S.J. 1993. *Creative Partnerships: Librarians and Teachers Working Together*. Worthington, OH: Linworth.

Foerstel, Herbert N. 2002. *Banned in the U.S.A.: A Reference Guide to Book Censorship in Schools and Public Libraries*. Westport, CT: Greenwood Press.

Honnold, RoseMary. 2003. *101+ Teen Programs That Work*. New York: Neal-Schuman.

Honnold, RoseMary. 2005. *More Teen Programs That Work*. New York: Neal-Schuman.

Jones, Patrick, Michele Gorman, and Tricia Suellentrop. 2004. *Connecting Young Adults and Libraries: A How-To-Do-It Manual for Librarians*. New York: Neal-Schuman.

Jones, Patrick, Maureen L. Hartman, and Patricia Taylor. 2006. *Connecting with Reluctant Teen Readers: Tips, Titles, and Tools*. New York: Neal-Schuman.

Figure 18.2. C.L.A.S.S. Rave Card

Celebrating National Library Card Sign Up Month with C.L.A.S.S.

<LIBRARY LOGO>   **&**   <SCHOOL DISTRICT LOGO>

Connecting Libraries And Schools Simultaneously

Get the most important school supply of all a FREE Public Library Card

To make arrangements for sign language interpretation, please call <PHONE/TDD NUMBERS> at least 48 hours in advance.

Jones, Patrick and Joel Shoemaker. 2001. *Do It right! Best Practices for Serving Young Adults in School and Public Libraries.* New York: Neal-Schuman.

Ott, Valerie A. 2006. *Teen Programs with Punch: A Month-by-Month Guide.* Westport, CT: Libraries Unlimited.

Peterson, Jean Sunde. 2007. *The Essential Guide to Talking with Teens: Ready-to-Use Discussions for School and Youth Groups.* Minneapolis: Free Spirit.

Simpson, Martha Seif and Lucretia I. Duwel. 2007. *Bringing Classes into the Public Library: A Handbook for Librarians.* Jefferson, NC: McFarland & Co.

Walter, Virginia A. and Elaine E. Meyers. 2003. *Teens & Libraries: Getting It Right.* Chicago: American Library Association.

Step 7: Set Up the Program Area

There is no one area where this will take place.

Step 8: Conduct the Event

Follow the prepared agenda.

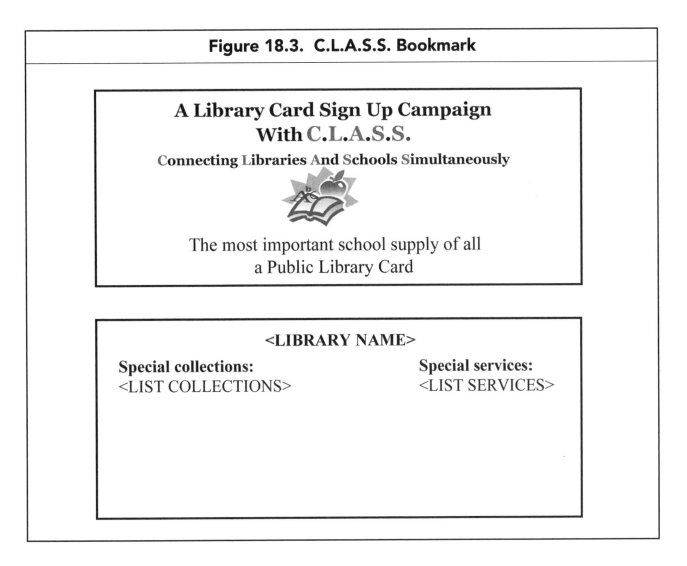

Figure 18.3. C.L.A.S.S. Bookmark

Step 9: Evaluate the Program

Evaluations are helpful for planning future programs. Customize the evaluation form from Part I (see Figure I.3 on CD) for participants to fill out. Collect the forms as the audience leaves.

19
FAMILY AFFAIR—
AN ORAL HISTORY PROJECT

PROGRAM DESCRIPTION

A family history is more than family trees and charts with names and dates. It is also the stories passed from generation to generation. Learning to develop and conduct an oral history interview will help teens collect these stories from their family members. Teens can record the interviews on audio or videotape and make a treasure of their family heritage.

PROGRAM GOALS

The Oral History Project will connect teens with the older generations of their families while also encouraging them to become library users. The teen conducting the interview can deepen his or her relationship with other members of the family and develop an understanding of his or her own identity. This program supports teens with love, care, and attention (Developmental Assets® #1–6), empowers them with opportunities to make a difference in their family and community (Developmental Assets #7–10), helps teens find activities that make constructive use of their time (Developmental Assets #17–20), and helps them develop life skills and social competencies (Developmental Assets #32–36).

HOW TO DO IT

Step 1: Make a Plan

Instructions and information will be presented to the Teen Advisory Board (TAB) at the meetings, and family members are welcome to attend. The TAB members conduct the interviews with their families on their own time. The teens will use their recording equipment. Refreshments can be served during the meetings.

An alternative plan is to invite the teens with their family members to come to the library to make podcast recordings. The recordings can be posted on the library's Web site during related community celebrations. Easy instructions for making a podcast can be found online at www.sweetwater.com/feature/podcasting/howto.php.

Step 2: Set a Date, Book a Space

The informational presentations take place during two or more TAB meetings to help teens learn more about genealogy and oral history interviews. The teens will conduct the interviews on their time.

Step 3: Book the Presenter

Invite a representative from your library's genealogy or local history department to speak at the first meeting and lead a tour of the local history department. Invite the chairperson of a local genealogical society to speak at the next meeting.

Step 4: Create a Program Format and Agenda

This is a sample agenda for the meetings. Adapt it for your needs.

10:30	Welcome, announcements and introductions
10:40	Guest speaker
11:00	Tour genealogy/local history department
11:30	Work on interviewing techniques
12:30	End of session

Step 5: Market the Program

Announce the project at a TAB meeting. Post flyers (see Figure 19.1) in the library and around the teen center.

Step 6: Gather Materials

Create a handout explaining the steps involved in preparing for and conducting an oral history interview. An example is provided in Figure 19.2.

Book List

Annal, David. 2005. *Easy Family History: The Stress-free Guide to Starting Your Research*. London: National Archives.

Best, Laura. 2005. *Scrapbooking Your Family History*. New York: Sterling.

Darrow, Carol Cook and Susan Winchester. 2007. *The Genealogist's Guide to Researching Tax Records*. Westminster, MD: Heritage Books.

Davis, John Rivard. 1993. *Not Merely Ancestors: A Guide to Teaching Genealogy in the Schools*. Baltimore: Clearfield Company.

Hull, Lise. 2006. *Tracing Your Family History: The Complete Guide to Locating Your Ancestors and Finding Out Where You Came From*. Pleasantville, NY: Reader's Digest.

Koons, Bee Bartron. 2004. *Teaching Genealogy to Young People*. Westminster, MD: Willow Bend Books.

Koons, Bee Bartron. 2004. *Young People's Workbook for Junior Genealogy Classes*. Westminster, MD: Willow Bend Books.

Melnyk, Marcia Yannizze. 2005. *Family History 101: A Beginner's Guide to Finding Your Ancestors*. Cincinnati: Family Tree Books.

Otterson, Michael. 2006. *Finding Your Family on the Internet: The Ultimate Guide to Online Family History Research*. Sandy, UT: Silverleaf Press.

Powell, Kimberly and William G. Hartley. 2006. *The Everything Family Tree Book: Research and Preserve Your Family History*. Avon, MA: Adams Media.

Renick, Barbara. 2003. *Genealogy 101: How to Trace Your Family's History and Heritage*. Nashville: Rutledge Hill Press.

Figure 19.1. Oral History Project Publicity Flyer

It's a
"Family Affair—Oral History Project"

**Come Join the Teen Advisory Board
<DATE AND TIME> at <LOCATION>
to Learn How to Turn Your Family Stories into
Family Treasures!**

Bring your Tape Recorders and Camcorders!

Learn how to develop and conduct an oral interview.

For more information contact
<CONTACT NAME, PHONE NUMBER, AND E-MAIL ADDRESS>.

<LIBRARY LOGO>

To make arrangements for sign-language interpretation, call
<PHONE/TDD NUMBERS> at least 48 hours in advance.

**Figure 19.2. Guidelines for Developing and Conducting
an Oral History Interview**

Guidelines for Developing and Conducting
an Oral History Interview

A filing system should be developed to ensure your oral history materials are organized so that the recordings will be easily accessible. This will be a tremendous help to your family and future generations.

- Before beginning an interview with a family member, it is important to assemble some basic data. Usually information is found in family papers, family bibles, etc. This information will assist you in determining the topics for your family member to include when telling their stories.

- After conducting background research, determine a focus for the interview. Interviews may fall under three general categories: (1) the impact of a main historical event or trend, (2) the relationship with various aspects of social life, and (3) the structure and dynamics of family life itself. In addition, it is also possible to just record family stories, traditions, customs, or beliefs.

- The first interviews you conduct should be with close family members who enjoy discussing the past. This allows you to get familiar with conducting interviews with people who will be easy to interview.

- In addition to recording the interview on audiotape, videotape, etc., you should make a written record. Include things such as the date and location of the interview, the person conducting the interview and the person giving the interview, and a brief summary of the subjects covered. Include a copy of the interview questions or the topic list.

- Conduct the interview in a place favorable to conversation and free of a lot of noise. You should be able to make good eye contact and clearly hear the person you are interviewing. The ideal positioning is sitting across from each other, with the recording device properly placed. The setting of the interview should also be free from distractions such as a telephone if possible.

- It is important to remind the interviewee of what you would like him or her to discuss. You may plan for this by discussing in advance what he or she would like to talk about. You should guide the interviewee along with your questions, but do not hinder the person. Ask open-ended questions. Also, make sure the questions you ask are impartial. For example, do not begin a question with "Don't you agree that . . ." Be sure to let the interviewee finish a question before asking another one. It is difficult to plan for the amount of time necessary, but you should minimally plan to have enough recording materials (cassettes or tapes) for several hours.

Renick, Barbara and Richard S. Wilson. 1998. *The Internet for Genealogists: A Beginner's Guide*. La Habra, CA: Compuology.

Stephenson, Lynda Rutledge. 2000. *The Complete Idiot's Guide to Writing Your Family History*. Indianapolis: Alpha.

Swan, James. 2004. *The Librarian's Guide to Genealogical Services and Research*. New York: Neal-Schuman.

Taylor, Maureen Alice. 2005. *Uncovering Your Ancestry Through Family Photographs*. Cincinnati: Family Tree Books.

Warren, Paula Stuart and James W. Warren. 2001. *Your Guide to the Family History Library*. Cincinnati: Betterway Books.

Step 7: Set Up the Program Area

Set up chairs in the teen area of the library. Prepare simple refreshments for each meeting like soft drinks and trail mix.

Step 8: Conduct the Event

Follow the prepared agenda.

Step 9: Evaluate the Program

Evaluations are helpful for planning future programs. Customize the evaluation form from Part I (see Figure I.3 on CD) for participants to fill out. Collect the forms as the audience leaves.

20
MISSION POSSIBLE: SPY A BOOK

PROGRAM DESCRIPTION

Mission Possible: Spy a Book (a summer reading program) is a systemwide scavenger hunt designed to encourage teens to visit all of the branches in the public library system. The mission, if they choose to accept it, is to journey to each branch location and collect a puzzle piece. Teens are eligible for a grand prize drawing when they have visited each branch and completed the puzzle.

If you are in a smaller library system or there is only one library in your area, design your scavenger hunt to encourage teens to visit different departments or areas in your library or businesses in your area to collect a puzzle piece. To participate, local businesses donate the door prizes.

PROGRAM GOALS

The scavenger hunt is an activity based on a list of questions to be answered and objects to be collected. Some answers and objects can be collected at specific locations; others can be collected at numerous locations. The questions are in random order. It is an active way for teens to get to know library branch locations or different departments in your library. This program supports teens with love, care, and attention (Developmental Assets® #1–6) and nurtures in them a commitment to learning (Developmental Assets #21–25).

HOW TO DO IT

Step 1: Make a Plan

The hunt can be part of the summer reading program. Figures 20.1 and 20.2 show sample letters to the library branches explaining the program.

Schedule a meeting with the marketing director of a local bus company if your community has public transportation. Teens will need transportation to travel around the city. Partnering with a bus company can have many benefits, such as free publicity for the library. The library logo can be used on bus stop signage and on buses; the library's location can be printed on bus schedules. Further collaboration is possible for other events: free bus passes for teens during Teen Read Week in October, for example.

The cost may vary depending on the prizes and incentives. Purchase or collect prizes for drawings at the final celebration. Request funds to buy refreshments for the final celebration. Pizza and soft drinks would be nice for teens.

Figure 20.1. Mission Possible Presentation Letter to Branch Libraries

Mission Possible Presentation Letter to Branch Libraries

<LIBRARY LOGO>

<DATE>

Dear Fellow Special Agents:

By now you should have received both parts of the Mystery Puzzle at your Headquarters. You should have the puzzle pieces designated for your specific Branch and the "Mission Possible" instruction form/map. You will need a container of some sort to keep the puzzle pieces in. <CONTACT NAME> will supply the badges described on the form, at a later date.

How to Handle the Puzzle Pieces

This activity is designed to encourage teens to visit all of the branches in the <LIBRARY NAME> system. Those wishing to participate must register at their local branch. They will receive an instruction form/map, one piece of the puzzle, and a secret agent badge. The badge will say "Spy a Book * <LIBRARY INITIALS>."

Staff must fill in the top right-hand corner that asks for "Spy Code #" and "Headquarters." The "Spy Code #" will be any number assigned at your discretion, following the 00- ; "Headquarters" will be your branch name or initials. Keep a list of participants' names and "Spy Code #s" so they may not be duplicated at your location.

Because this is a systemwide scavenger hunt, teens from all over the city may be coming to your library to participate. Their badge will indicate that they are on a "Mission." Please give them 1 (one) puzzle piece per participant. To complete the Mystery Puzzle, they must travel to all of the branches in the <LIBRARY NAME> system.

Participants must return to the branch where they registered in order to be entered into the Grand Prize Drawing. Upon presenting you with a completed puzzle, they are to receive a token gift from the library and/or <PARTICIPATING ORGANIZATIONS' NAMES>. Their name and "Spy Code #" will then be submitted for the Grand Prize Drawing. Please use their Summer Reading Program Registration/Entry Form. Write their "Spy Code # (SC#)" in the top left-hand corner. For "Activity completed" put "Mystery Puzzle." These forms should be kept separate. There will be a Grand Prize Drawing held at each branch at the conclusion of the Summer Reading Program in <MONTH>. The <PARTICIPATING ORGANIZATIONS' NAMES> along with the <LIBRARY NAME> will provide the Grand Prizes. You will receive these gifts shortly. Let participants know that the winner will be notified by telephone. If you have any questions please contact Special Agent <CONTACT NAME, PHONE NUMBER, AND E-MAIL ADDRESS>.

Thank you for your commitment and service to the cause.

Special Agent,

<CONTACT NAME AND TITLE>
<LIBRARY NAME AND ADDRESS>
<PHONE NUMBER>
<E-MAIL ADDRESS>

Figure 20.2. Mission Possible Follow-Up Letter to Branch Libraries

Mission Possible Follow-Up Letter to Branch Libraries

<LIBRARY LOGO>

<DATE>

Dear Fellow Special Agents:

As promised previously, <CONTACT NAME> has secured the badges for the Mystery Puzzle scavenger hunt. There should be enough in your shipment to give one button to each staff member. This is a great promotional tool for the Summer Reading Program.

The remaining badges are for the teens participating in the Mystery Puzzle Scavenger Hunt who register at your headquarters.

To activate the buttons, remove the small black protective covering and close the pin. Always remember to unlatch the pin when not in use to save on batteries. (Please pass this information on to participants.)

Again, this activity is designed to encourage teens to visit all of the branches in the <LIBRARY NAME> system. Those wishing to participate must register at their local branch. They will receive an instruction form/map, one piece of the puzzle, and a Secret Agent Badge. Teens from all over the city may be coming to your library to participate. By wearing a badge, teens indicate that they are on a "Mission." You should, at that time, provide them with 1 (one) puzzle piece.

Most agencies will receive 50 badges. If you think that's more than you will need or if you need more, please contact <CONTACT NAME, PHONE NUMBER, AND E-MAIL ADDRESS>. Return your extra badges so we may redistribute them to the branches that need more.

Special Agent,

<CONTACT NAME AND TITLE>
<LIBRARY NAME AND ADDRESS>
<PHONE NUMBER>
<E-MAIL ADDRESS>

Step 2: Set a Date, Book a Space

Start the scavenger hunt at the beginning of the summer reading program, and end it at the conclusion of the program. Schedule a date for the final party.

Step 3: Book the Presenter

Contact the local public transit company, the library branches, and/or local businesses and obtain commitments to participate.

Step 4: Create a Program Format and Agenda

The final celebration is a party hosted by the Teen Advisory Board (TAB) with music and refreshments. You might also invite a local storyteller to perform. Hold a prize drawing at the end of the party. Encourage the TAB members to bring guests to promote new membership.

Step 5: Market the Program

Add the scavenger hunt to the flyers and rave cards already being produced by the summer reading program committee to advertise the events. Include it in the summer reading program press release. Contact teen organizations such as the Boys & Girls Clubs, the YMCA, and homeschoolers' organizations.

Step 6: Gather Materials

Make sure each participating location has instruction forms/maps (see Figure 20.3) and secret agent badges to give to the teens when they register for the hunt. Send the puzzle base (see Figures 20.4 and 20.5), pieces, and secret agent log (see Figure 20.6) to the participating branches, departments, or businesses. Each location should receive a piece designated for that location only. (For a sample completed puzzle, see Figure 20.7.) To play up the spy theme, spy fiction can be featured in displays, book talks, and book lists.

Book List

Anderson, Sheila B. 2004. *Serving Older Teens.* Westport, CT: Libraries Unlimited.

Anderson, Sheila B. 2005. *Extreme Teens: Library Services to Nontraditional Young Adults.* Westport, CT: Libraries Unlimited.

Anderson, Sheila B. 2007. *Serving Young Teens and 'Tweens.* Westport, CT: Libraries Unlimited.

Burgett, Gordon. 2001. *Treasure and Scavenger Hunts: How to Plan, Create, and Give Them.* Santa Maria, CA: Communication Unlimited.

Churchill, E. Richard. 1968. *Fun with American Literature.* Nashville: Abingdon Press.

Edwards, Kirsten. 2002. *Teen Library Events: A Month-by-Month Guide.* Westport, CT: Greenwood Press.

Honnold, RoseMary. 2005. *More Teen Programs That Work.* New York: Neal-Schuman.

Jones, Patrick and Joel Shoemaker. 2001. *Do It Right! Best Practices for Serving Young Adults in School and Public Libraries.* New York: Neal-Schuman.

Mahood, Kristine. 2006. *A Passion for Print: Promoting Reading and Books to Teens.* Westport, CT: Libraries Unlimited.

Figure 20.3. Mission Possible Instructions and Map

Mission Possible Instructions and Map

Name: _____   Spy Code #: _____00-_____

Age: _____   Headquarters: _____

Phone #: _____

MISSION POSSIBLE: Spy a Book

Your mission, should you choose to accept it, is to journey to each <LIBRARY NAME> location to collect a puzzle piece. When you register for the Teen Summer Reading Program you will be given a badge and a number. This number will serve as your **SPY CODE NUMBER**. Once you have traveled to all locations completing the puzzle, return to your Headquarters (the library where you are registered). Upon presenting the completed puzzle, you will receive a token of appreciation for a job well done, and your **SPY CODE NUMBER** will be entered in a drawing for a Grand Prize.

Below you will find a map of all the library locations. You can get to them by bus, with your parents, or on your own. On the back of this sheet is a grid where you can glue your puzzle pieces as you collect them for safekeeping. **Only completed puzzles will be eligible for a Grand Prize Drawing.** Your assignment will begin on <DATE>. Deadline for entries will be no later than <TIME AND DATE>. Drawing will take place on <DATE>.

And, as always, if you are caught **"Spying a Book,"** this agency **will claim** any and all knowledge of your existence. (This page **will not** self-destruct in 5 seconds.)

<INSERT YOUR MAP AND BRANCH LOCATION KEY HERE>

Sample Map and Branch Location Key (Fort Worth Public Library in Texas)

(1)   **Central**—500 W. 3rd Street
(2)   **East Regional**—6301 Bridge Street
(3)   **Southwest Regional**—4001 Library Lane
(4)   **BOLD**—Butler Housing Comm.
(5)   **COOL**—5060 Avenue G,
(6)   **Diamond Hill/Jarvis**—1300 NE 35th St.
(7)   **East Berry**—4300 East Berry Street
(8)   **Meadowbrook**—5651 E. Lancaster Ave.
(9)   **Northside**—601 Park Street
(10) **Ridglea**—3628 Bernie Anderson Dr.
(11) **Riverside**—2913 Yucca Avenue
(12) **Seminary South**—501 E. Bolt Street
(13) **Shamblee**—959 E. Rosedale Street
(14) **Summerglen**—4205 Basswood Blvd.
(15) **Wedgwood**—3816 Kimberly Lane

Figure 20.4. Mission Possible Puzzle Base

1	2	3	4	5
6	7	8	9	10
11	12	13	14	15

Figure 20.5. Mission Possible Sample Puzzle with Starter Piece

	2	3	4	5
6	7	8	9	10
11	12	13	14	15

| Figure 20.6. Mission Possible Secret Agent Log |||
| **Mission Possible Secret Agent Log** |||
	Agent Name	**Spy Code #**	**Phone #**
1.			
2.			
3.			
4.			
5.			
6.			
7.			
8.			
9.			
10.			
11.			
12.			
13.			
14.			
15.			
16.			
17.			
18.			
19.			
20.			

Figure 20.7. Mission Possible Completed Sample Puzzle

Mondowney, JoAnn G. 2001. *Hold Them in Your Heart: Successful Strategies for Library Services to At-Risk Teens*. New York: Neal-Schuman.

Nichols, C. Allen. 2004. *Thinking Outside the Book: Alternatives for Today's Teen Library Collections*. Westport, CT: Libraries Unlimited.

Speirs, John. 1999. *Best Christmas Hunt Ever*. New York: Scholastic.

Travis, Falcon. 1993. *Great Book of Whodunit Puzzles: Mini-Mysteries for You to Solve*. New York: Sterling.

Washington Post. 1984. *The Book Bag Treasury of Literary Quizzes*. New York: Scribner.

Spy Fiction Book List

Avi and Karina Raude, illus. 2007. *The Traitors' Gate*. New York: Atheneum Books for Young Readers.

Carter, Ally. 2006. *I'd Tell You I Love You, but Then I'd Have to Kill You*. New York: Hyperion Books for Children.

Carter, Ally. 2007. *Cross My Heart and Hope to Spy*. New York: Hyperion.

Carter, Ally and Renée Raudman. 2007. *Cross My Heart and Hope to Spy*. Grand Haven, MI: Brilliance Audio.

Greenland, Shannon. 2008. *The Winning Element*. New York: Speak.

Harlow, Joan Hiatt. 2005. *Midnight Rider*. New York: Margaret K. McElderry Books.

Higgins, Jack and Justin Richards. 2006. *Sure Fire*. New York: G.P. Putnam's Sons.

Higson, Charles. 2007. *Double or Die: A James Bond Adventure*. New York: Hyperion Books for Children.

Horowitz, Anthony. 2006. *Ark Angel*. New York: Philomel Books.

Horowitz, Anthony. 2006. *Point Blank*. New York: Speak.

Horowitz, Anthony. 2007. *Snakehead*. New York: Philomel Books.

Horowitz, Anthony, Emil Fortune, and John David Lawson. 2006. *Alex Rider: The Gadgets*. New York: Philomel Books.

Jolley, Dan. 2007. *The Vosarak Code*. Los Angeles: TOKYOPOP.

Mason, Adrienne and Pat Cupples. 2008. *Secret Spies*. Toronto: Kids Can Press.

McNab, Andy and Robert Rigby. 2006. *Payback*. New York: Putnam.

McNab, Andy and Robert Rigby. 2007. *Meltdown: The Final Chapter of the Watts Family Adventures!* New York: G.P. Putnam's Sons.

Plum-Ucci, Carol. 2008. *Streams of Babel*. Orlando: Harcourt.

Ransom, Candice F. and Greg Call, illus. 2007. *Signals in the Sky*. Renton, WA: Mirrorstone.

Reeve, Philip and David Wyatt, illus. 2007. *Starcross (OR) The Coming of the Moobs! (OR) Our Adventures in the Fourth Dimension!* New York: Bloomsbury Children's Books.

Simmons, Michael. 2006. *The Rise of Lubchenko*. New York: Razorbill.

Step 7: Set Up the Program Area

Make sure that all library branches have the necessary game pieces and information easily accessible.

Step 8: Conduct the Event

Host the final celebration with prize drawings and refreshments at the end of the summer reading program.

Step 9: Evaluate the Program

Evaluations are helpful for planning future programs. Customize the evaluation form from Part I (see Figure I.3 on CD) for participants to fill out. Collect the forms as the audience leaves.

Chapter 5

OUTSIDE THE BOX: SOMETHING DIFFERENT

21
CHECK IT OUT @ THE LIBRARY
(TEEN CABLE SHOW)

PROGRAM DESCRIPTION

Check It Out is a teen cable program hosted by the library and a local cable station. The taped program is aired numerous times throughout the month, at the discretion of the cable station. The taping is done once a month in advance, after school and/or on the weekend. The program addresses teen issues and highlights local teen talent, including singers, dancers and bands, poets, and comedians, as well as features a monthly book review.

PROGRAM GOALS

The cable show gives teens a forum to address interests and concerns and serves as a means of communication, a gathering place that unites the teen community for networking, learning, and collaboration. The program also increases awareness of the library among teens and their families. Check It Out supports teens with love, care, and attention (Developmental Assets® #1–6), empowers teens with opportunities to make a difference in their family and community (Developmental Assets #7–10), establishes clear boundaries and has high expectations (Developmental Assets #11–16), helps teens find activities that make constructive use of their time (Developmental Assets #17–20), instills positive values to guide them (Developmental Assets #26–31), helps them develop life skills and social competencies (Developmental Assets #32–36), and nurtures, celebrates, and affirms their positive identity (Developmental Assets #37–40).

HOW TO DO IT

Step 1: Make a Plan

Set up a meeting with the cable administrator and/or the production manager to approve the production of the show and to set up a schedule for filming. One to three members of the Teen Advisory Board (TAB) can host the show. It is not necessary to have the same members hosting each month.

Line up special guests to interview. Ask the guests to submit a list of ten questions that they would like the teens to ask them. Members of the TAB are also encouraged to ask questions that interest them. Select local talent to showcase, such as singers, dancers and bands, poets, artists, and comedians. All works must be original to avoid copyright issues. Choose a book, video, CD, or DVD that is owned by the library to be reviewed and discussed each month.

The show is set up similar to *The View*. It is helpful for the TAB members to watch a few episodes of the Hot Topics portion of the program to see how the speakers look at the camera and not at their notes. Review a taping of the previous month's show during TAB meetings to see how the program can be improved.

Step 2: Set a Date, Book a Space

Begin taping one month before the first program is to air. Set a regular day and time for training and planning the program and another day for taping each month after school or on weekends. The filming can take place in the teen section of your library or at the cable station and tape on location at special events.

Step 3: Book the Presenter

For each show, schedule three teens and invite special guests for interviews and performances.

Step 4: Create a Program Format and Agenda

The following agenda represents a typical 30-minute cable program. Adjust it to fit your time and number of performers.

- Hot Topics—Discussion by TAB Members and Special Guest Interview: Individuals or groups with issues or concerns of interest to teens are showcased. For example, a financial aid counselor discusses funding for college or a local businessman discusses entrepreneurship. (There are usually two special guest interviews per show.)
- Home Grown Talent Showcase: The segment features local talent, such as singers, dancers, bands, poets, and comedians.
- Monthly Book Review/Book Talk: A different TAB member each month leads a five-minute book talk.
- Closing Remarks: A TAB member recaps the show by thanking the special guests, the local talent, and the members who conducted the interviews and book talk. End each show by inviting the TV audience to "Check it out at the library."

Step 5: Market the Program

Post the show schedule on the cable station and on the library's Web page. Send out a press release (see Figure 21.1).

Step 6: Gather Materials

All teens and guests who appear in the show must first sign a release form (see Figure 21.2). Make sure the teens have a supply.

Figure 21.1. Check It Out Cable Show Press Release

Check It Out Cable Show Press Release

<LIBRARY LOGO>

NEWS RELEASE
<DATE>
FOR IMMEDIATE RELEASE

<LIBRARY NAME>
Teen Advisory Board Cable Show

The Teen Advisory Board of the <LIBRARY NAME> will host a teen talk/variety show called "Check It Out @ the Library." The show is sponsored by <LIBRARY NAME> in conjunction with the <CITY COUNCIL> and <CITY CABLE STATION>.

Programs address teen issues, highlight local teen talent, and feature a monthly book review. The show runs on <CITY CABLE CHANNEL> at the following times starting <DATE>:

Day	Time
Sunday	
Monday	
Tuesday	
Wednesday	
Thursday	
Friday	
Saturday	

All those interested in becoming involved are asked to join the <LIBRARY NAME> Teen Advisory Board. We meet <DATE AND TIME> in <LOCATION>.

Contact person:

<CONTACT NAME AND TITLE>
<LIBRARY NAME AND ADDRESS>
<PHONE NUMBER>
<E-MAIL ADDRESS>

Figure 21.2. Check It Out Cable Show Television Release Form

Check It Out Cable Show
Television Release Form

\<CABLE STATION NAME\>
\<CONTACT NAME\>
\<ADDRESS\>
\<PHONE NUMBER\>

RELEASE FOR COMMUNITY CABLE TELEVISION

Permission is hereby granted for the use of my image and/or voice, or the image and/or voice of a minor child or children, or group of individuals to be videotaped and cable cast over \<CITY\>'s Community Cable Television Channels \<CHANNEL NUMBER(S)\> in the \<CITY/STATE\>.

Date of Event: _____

Event: _____

Individual or Group Name: _____

Signature: _____
               (Signature of parent or guardian of minor child)

This release must be received prior to the event being taped.

Book List

Alexander, George. 2003. *Why We Make Movies: Black Filmmakers Talk About the Magic of Cinema.* New York: Harlem Moon.

Baldwin, Chris. 2003. *Stage Directing.* Wiltshire, England: Crowood Press.

Caldwell, Sara C. 2005. *Jumpstart Your Awesome Film Production Company.* New York: Allworth Press.

Cury, Ivan. 2007. *Directing and Producing for Television: A Format Approach.* Boston: Focal Press.

Dean, Peter. 2002. *Production Management: Making Shows Happen.* Wiltshire, England: Crowood Press.

Fantasia, Louis. 2002. *Instant Shakespeare: A Proven Technique for Actors, Directors, and Teachers.* Chicago: Ivan R. Dee.

Friedman, Lise and Mary Dowdle. 2002. *Break a Leg! The Kids' Book of Acting and Stagecraft*. New York: Workman.

Gilles, D.B. 2005. *The Portable Film School: Everything You'd Learn in Film School (Without Ever Going to Class)*. New York: St. Martin's Griffin.

Holden, Tom. 2002. *Film Making*. London: Hodder Headline.

Noronha, Shonan F.R. 2003. *Opportunities in Television and Video Careers*. Chicago: VGM Career Books.

O'Brien, Lisa and Stephen MacEachern, illus. 2007. *Lights, Camera, Action! Making Movies and TV from the Inside Out*. Toronto: Maple Tree Press.

Patz, Deborah S. 2002. *Production Management, 101: The Ultimate Guide to Film and Television Production Management and Coordination*. Studio City, CA: M. Wiese Productions.

Seger, Linda and Edward Jay Whetmore. 2004. *From Script to Screen: The Collaborative Art of Filmmaking*. Los Angeles: Lone Eagle.

Steiff, Josef. 2005. *The Complete Idiot's Guide to Independent Filmmaking*. New York: Alpha.

Tirard, Laurent. 2002. *Moviemakers' Master Class: Private Lessons from the World's Foremost Directors*. New York: Faber and Faber.

Wolsky, Tom. 2005. *Video Production Workshop*. San Francisco: CMP Books.

Step 7: Set Up the Program Area

The cable studio will have all the production equipment needed. Bring notes for the interviews. Have the performers bring any special props they may need.

Step 8: Conduct the Event

Try to give as many members as you can something to do during the production of the show so that all members can feel ownership of the program. For example:

- Three teen members discuss Hot Topics.
- The same three members interview a guest.
- One to two members introduce and interview the talent.
- One member conducts the book review/book talk.
- One member gives the closing remarks.
- All remaining members are a part of the audience.

Step 9: Evaluate the Program

Evaluations are helpful for planning future programs. To get suggestions for future shows, and to help publicize the program, place numerous copies of the Check It Out @ the Library Viewer Questionnaire (see Figure 21.3) at the library check-out desks.

Figure 21.3. Check It Out @ the Library Viewer Questionnaire

Check It Out @ the Library
Viewer Questionnaire

The purpose of the cable show is to promote <CITY/STATE> to teens and to increase library usage and awareness.

1. Do you have <CITY> cable service at home?   Yes / No

2. Have you ever watched "Check It Out @ the Library"
    a teen show hosted on <CHANNEL NUMBER>?   Yes / No

3. Did you enjoy the program?   Yes / No

4. Would you like to see more programs like this?   Yes / No

5. Did this program entice you to visit and/or check something   Yes / No
    out at the library?

6. Will you be using the library's many resources in the future?   Yes / No

7. Are you planning to watch our next production of   Yes / No
    "Check It Out @ The Library" on <CHANNEL NUMBER>?

8. Will you tell a friend?
                                                                                 Yes / No

Suggestions for future shows:

_____

_____

_____

General Comments:

_____

_____

_____

Please check one:

___ Youth   ___ Teen   ___ Adult

Thank You!

22
MAKEUP, MASSAGE, AND A MESSAGE: A MOTHER–DAUGHTER DAY OUT

PROGRAM DESCRIPTION

Mothers and daughters enjoy an afternoon of pampering with cosmetic consultants and local massage therapists and hear a dynamic message. Whether a mom invites her daughter or vice versa, this is a treat every lady deserves.

PROGRAM GOALS

The Mother–Daughter Day Out is an opportunity for the library to establish partnerships with local businesses, increase library awareness among women and girls, and foster good relationships between mothers and daughters. The program supports teen girls with love, care, and attention (Developmental Assets® #1–6) and establishes clear boundaries and has high expectations (Developmental Assets #11–16).

HOW TO DO IT

Step 1: Make a Plan

Request a grant to pay for refreshments. Work in partnership with beauty consultants and massage therapists. Invite them to participate in your pampering day by having a make-over party in your library. Most consultants and therapists will be happy to do so, as it gives them an opportunity to make new contacts and distribute their information. Contact a woman's organization such as the Breast Cancer Society, and help them get their message out by inviting them to send a speaker.

Step 2: Set a Date, Book a Space

Mother–Daughter Day Out is a great way to celebrate National Women's History Month on a Saturday in March. An auditorium or a meeting room set up lecture style works best for the speaker portion of the program. Talk with the beauty consultant and massage therapist about what kind of space and setup they need.

Step 3: Book the Presenter

Contact a beauty consultant (Mary Kay or Fashion Flair, for example) and a massage therapist or a cosmetology school and a massage therapy school. They can bring their products and their chairs to perform a five-minute introductory massage. Select and book a speaker to provide the message, a speaker who will deliver a message that will hold the audience's attention because they are there for pampering, not lecturing. With all this pampering, however, it is important also to have a strong message.

Step 4: Create a Program Format and Agenda

Schedule the message first on the agenda to ensure attendance for the guest speaker. The makeup and massage can be done simultaneously at the end of the program.

Step 5: Market the Program

Produce rave cards and flyers (see Figures 22.1 and 22.2) to advertise the event, and distribute them at schools, churches, and homeschooler and senior citizens organizations. Distribute rave cards to local businesses and restaurants. Post flyers at daycare centers and apartment complexes.

Step 6: Gather Materials

Display books that would be of interest to women: health, beauty, and fashion. As always, one must have a library card to participate; therefore, make library card sign-up available at the door.

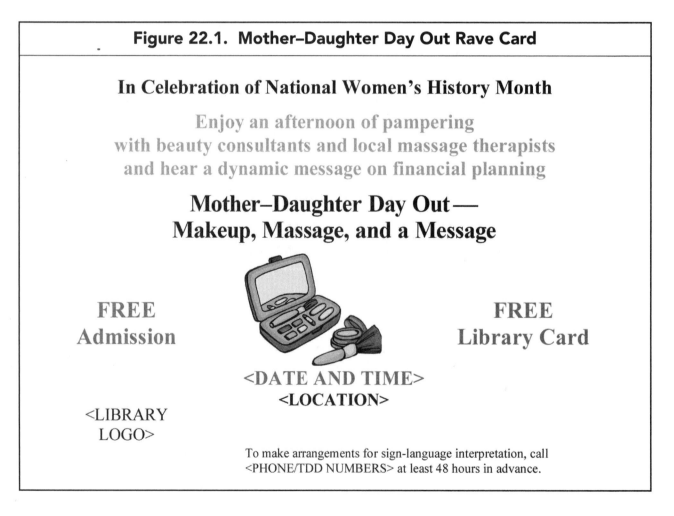

Figure 22.1. Mother–Daughter Day Out Rave Card

In Celebration of National Women's History Month

Enjoy an afternoon of pampering
with beauty consultants and local massage therapists
and hear a dynamic message on financial planning

**Mother–Daughter Day Out—
Makeup, Massage, and a Message**

FREE
Admission

FREE
Library Card

<DATE AND TIME>
<LOCATION>

<LIBRARY
LOGO>

To make arrangements for sign-language interpretation, call
<PHONE/TDD NUMBERS> at least 48 hours in advance.

Figure 22.2. Mother–Daughter Day Out Publicity Flyer

In Celebration of National Women's History Month

Enjoy an afternoon of pampering
with beauty consultants and local massage therapists
and hear a dynamic message on financial planning

Mother–Daughter Day Out— Makeup, Massage, and a Message

FREE
Admission

FREE
Library Card Sign-Up
Available at the Door

\<DATE AND TIME\>
\<LOCATION\>

\<LIBRARY
LOGO\>

To make arrangements for sign-language interpretation, call
\<PHONE/TDD NUMBERS\> at least 48 hours in advance.

Book List

Ashley, Martin. 2006. *Massage: A Career at Your Fingertips: The Complete Guide to Becoming a Bodywork Professional.* Somers, NY: Enterprise.

Begoun, Paula and Bryon Barron. 2008. *Don't Go to the Cosmetics Counter Without Me: A Unique Guide to Thousands of Skin-Care and Cosmetic Products, Plus the Latest Research on Keeping Skin Beautiful at Every Age.* Renton, WA: Beginning Press.

Bell-Scott, Patricia. 1991. *Double Stitch: Black Women Write About Mothers & Daughters.* Boston: Beacon Press.

Davidson, Cathy N. and E.M. Broner. 1980. *The Lost Tradition: Mothers and Daughters in Literature.* New York: F. Ungar.

Kearns, Caledonia. 1999. *Motherland: Writings by Irish American Women About Mothers and Daughters.* New York: W. Morrow.

Krasnow, Iris. 2006. *I Am My Mother's Daughter: Making Peace with Mom—Before It's Too Late.* New York: Basic Books.

Mumford, Susan. 2006. *The New Complete Guide to Massage.* New York: Plume Book.

O'Keefe, Adele. 2006. *The Official Guide to Body Massage.* London: Thomson.

Plumez, Jacqueline Hornor. 2002. *Mother Power: Discover the Difference That Women Have Made All Over the World.* Naperville, IL: Sourcebooks.

Stone, Victoria Jordan and Bob Shell. 2007. *The Complete Idiot's Guide to Massage Illustrated.* New York: Alpha.

Watson, Rosie. 2007. *Make-Up.* London: New Holland.

Yarosh, Daniel. 2008. *The New Science of Perfect Skin: Understanding Skin Care Myths and Miracles for Radiant Skin at Any Age.* New York: Broadway Books.

Step 7: Set Up the Program Area

Set up an area with chairs and tables for beauty consultants and massage therapists to perform. Set up the auditorium for the speaker to present the message. Prepare a place for refreshments.

Step 8: Conduct the Event

- Welcome and introductions
- Guest speaker
- Cosmetic demonstrations
- Massages
- Refreshments
- Wrap-up and thank-yous

Step 9: Evaluate the Program

Evaluations are helpful for planning future programs. Customize the evaluation form from Part I (see Figure I.3 on CD) for participants to fill out. Collect the forms as the audience leaves.

23
OLD SCHOOL TAKES NEW SCHOOL BACK TO SCHOOL PARTY

PROGRAM DESCRIPTION

The Old School Takes New School Back to School Party is a family affair consisting of a library scavenger hunt, a Swing Out dance demonstration and instructions, a Step Show, a school supplies give away, and door prizes. A library card is required for admission to the program.

PROGRAM GOALS

The Old School Takes New School Back to School Party is an opportunity to build community awareness of the library, support for families, and community involvement in improving education. Having family and community involved in a student's education makes a significant difference in learning. This program supports teens with love, care, and attention (Developmental Assets® #1–6) and nurtures in them a commitment to learning (Developmental Assets #21–25).

HOW TO DO IT

Step 1: Make a Plan

Coordinate with fraternities, sororities, community organizations, and businesses to renew their commitment to education by donating school supplies, prizes, and refreshments. Request a grant to pay for a DJ (approximately $150.00), and invite a radio station to broadcast on location. To be eligible for the free school supplies give away, participants must complete a Library Scavenger Hunt.

Step 2: Set a Date, Book a Space

Book a date in August before school starts—three hours on a Saturday afternoon. Book a large meeting room, a gallery, or other large open space in your library for the program.

Step 3: Book the Presenters

Hire a DJ to play old and current music for the program, and invite a radio station personality to emcee the event. Adult dance instructors from the community can demonstrate and teach swing dance, and a local step team or fraternity can do a step dance show. Dance lesson studios or a night club that offers Swing Out lessons are good resources for finding groups to lead the dance lessons. Representatives from the donating organizations and businesses hand out the school supplies and the donated door prizes.

Step 4: Create a Program Format and Agenda

- The DJ plays "old school" and "new school" music.
- Adult dance instructors demonstrate the Swing Out dance.
- A Step Team or fraternity members perform a Step Show routine.
- Dance instructors teach the Swing Out dance.
- Students participate in a Library Scavenger Hunt (parents are invited to join).
- Community organizations hand out school supplies.
- The program ends with door prize drawings.

Step 5: Market the Program

Create flyers and rave cards (see Figures 23.1 and 23.2) to advertise the event, and distribute them to the schools, the Boys & Girls Clubs, homeschoolers' organizations, local businesses, and restaurants. Post flyers at daycare centers and apartment complexes. Have Teen Advisory Board members distribute rave cards at popular teen hang-outs.

Step 6: Gather Materials

Put together packets of donated school supplies. Print scavenger hunt forms (see Figure 23.3). Gather simple refreshments, such as popcorn and soft drinks.

Book List

Bottomer, Paul. 2006. *Dance Class: How to Waltz, Quick Step, Foxtrot, Tango, Samba, Salsa, Merengue, Lambada and Line Dance—Step-by-Step!* London: Southwater.

Freese, Joan. 2008. *Hip-Hop Dancing.* Mankato, MN: Capstone Press.

Garofoli, Wendy. 2008. *Dance Team.* Mankato, MN: Capstone Press.

Garofoli, Wendy. 2008. *Modern Dance.* Mankato, MN: Snap Books.

Glass, Barbara S. 2007. *African American Dance: An Illustrated History.* Jefferson, NC: McFarland & Co.

Huntington, Carla Stalling. 2007. *Hip Hop Dance: Meanings and Messages.* Jefferson, NC: McFarland & Co.

King, Jamie. 2007. *Rock Your Body: The Ultimate Hip-Hop Inspired Workout to Slim, Shape, and Strengthen Your Body.* Emmaus, PA: Rodale.

Pagett, Matt. 2008. *The Best Dance Moves in the World—Ever! 100 New and Classic Moves and How to Bust Them.* San Francisco, CA: Chronicle Books LLC.

Phillips, Guy, Tasha Brown, and Cal Pozo. 2007. *Dancing with the Stars: Jive, Samba, and Tango Your Way Into the Best Shape of Your Life.* New York: Collins.

Pozo, Cal. 2007. *Let's Dance! The Complete Book and DVD of Ballroom Dance Instruction for Weddings, Parties, Fitness, and Fun.* New York: Hatherleigh Press.

Ramsey, Guthrie P. 2003. *Race Music: Black Cultures from Bebop to Hip-Hop.* Berkeley: University of California Press.

Shaw, Arnold. 1985. *Black Popular Music in America: From the Spirituals, Minstrels, and Ragtime to Soul, Disco, and Hip-Hop.* New York: Schirmer Books.

Figure 23.1. Back to School Party Publicity Flyer

<LIBRARY NAME>
Teen Advisory Board Presents

"Old School Takes New School Back to School Party!"

(Swing Out) (Step Show)

Admission . . . Show Library Card

**M.C.: <EMCEE NAME>
D.J.: <DJ NAME>**

School Supplies Donated by
<ORGANIZATION NAME(S)>

Refreshments and Door Prizes

When: <DATE AND TIME>
Where: <LOCATION>

<LIBRARY
LOGO>

To make arrangements for sign language interpretation, call
<PHONE/TDD NUMBERS> at least 48 hours in advance.

Figure 23.2. Back to School Party Rave Card

<LIBRARY NAME>

Teen Advisory Board

Presents

Must Show Library Card to Enter

School Supplies Giveaway

"Old School Takes New School Back to School Party"

When: <DATE AND TIME>

Where: <LOCATION>

(Swing Out)

(Step Show)

Refreshments

Door Prizes

<LIBRARY LOGO>

To make arrangements for sign language interpretation, call <PHONE/TDD NUMBERS> at least 48 hours in advance.

Short, Columbus, Meagan Good, Ne-Yo, and Darrin Dewitt Henson. 2007. *Stomp the Yard.* Culver City, CA: Sony Pictures Home Entertainment.

Step 7: Set Up the Program Area

Set up chairs for the performers and the audience. Set up the audio equipment and dance floor. Set up a table to distribute supplies. Have a box on hand to collect scavenger hunt entries for door prize drawings. Prepare a place for refreshments.

Step 8: Conduct the Event

Follow the prepared agenda.

Step 9: Evaluate the Program

Evaluations are helpful for planning future programs. Customize the evaluation form from Part I (see Figure I.3 on CD) for participants to fill out. Collect the forms as the audience leaves.

Figure 23.3. Back to School Party Library Scavenger Hunt Instructions

"Old School Takes New School Back to School" Party Library Scavenger Hunt Instructions

<LIBRARY LOGO>

LIBRARY SCAVENGER HUNT
For Students

Name:	Phone:
Address:	Grade:
School:	
E-mail:	

Rules: There are ten questions that will take you into all parts of the library. You do not have to work on the questions in order. You may work independently or in groups. You have 20 minutes to complete all ten questions.

Please return to the auditorium when done to receive a gift.

The first to complete the hunt will receive a prize! Good luck!

1. List two newspapers from areas outside the <CITY>'s area.

    (1) _____   (2) _____

2. Find books on college entrance tests such as the SAT or ACT. List the titles and call numbers of two books in the area.

    (1) _____   (2) _____

3. Locate the New Book Section. Name the title and author of a book that interests you.

    Title _____

    Author _____

(Cont'd.)

Figure 23.3. Back to School Party Library Scavenger Hunt Instructions
(Continued)

4. Find a PAC terminal (online catalog). List three ways of researching an item.

   a. _____

   b. _____

   c. _____

5. Browse through the fiction section. Find a book by an author whose last name starts with the same letter as your last name.

   Book Title _____

Author's last name	Your last name
_____	_____

6. In the foreign language section located in the Humanities Department, is there a book from your culture? If so, give the title of one book.

   Yes ___ No ___ Book Title _____

7. In the Genealogy Dept. find a high school annual; give the name of the school and the yearbook name.

   _____   _____

8. Locate the teen center. What is the theme of the decorations on the wall in that area?

   _____

9. Go to the youth center. Find the toy collection. Name two of the toys on display.

   (1) _____   (2) _____

10. Find the Media Department. Jot down the title of an audio book, a DVD, and a video that interest you.

    Audio Book: Title _____

    DVD: Title _____

    Video: Title _____

24
WORD-UP
(RADIO PROGRAM)

PROGRAM DESCRIPTION

Word-Up is a quarterly book discussion radio program broadcast out of the library to educate parents on how to help their teens use the library more effectively. Parents and other adults learn about the many available resources at the library so they can help guide teens and find helpful information for themselves.

PROGRAM GOALS

Word-Up is an innovative way to reach underserved communities and attract new users. The program is a collaboration between a local radio station and the library. The library will have free radio publicity, and the community will be encouraged to read and sign up for library cards. Word-Up supports teens with love, care, and attention (Developmental Assets® #1–6), empowers them with opportunities to make a difference in their family and community (Developmental Assets #7–10), and helps teens find activities that make constructive use of their time (Developmental Assets #17–20).

HOW TO DO IT

Step 1: Make a Plan

Local, school, or college radio stations may be interested in a new program. Meet with the radio station director and talk show host to decide whether the broadcast will be from the station or at the library location, the proposed dates for the broadcast, and the length of the program.

Step 2: Set a Date, Book a Space

As an example, our show airs live quarterly (July, October, January, April) on the second Sunday morning of the month for one hour, from 9:00 to 10:00 a.m., and each program is broadcast from a different library location. Provide a room with telephone access that could accommodate about five or six people (the talk show host, the other radio guests, and library staff personnel).

Step 3: Book the Presenter

Library staff who are comfortable talking about books, leading book discussions, and doing reader advisories would be most comfortable talking about books on air.

Step 4: Create a Program Format and Agenda

- Choose a book to be discussed.
- Select the next library location to announce during the program.
- Announce the next book, video, CD, or DVD that is owned by the library to be discussed next quarter, allowing the audience adequate time to read it.

Use the opportunity to publicize teen events, as well. Other topics for discussion might be resources for parenting teens or targeting teen parents as the audience, encouraging them to read to their babies.

Step 5: Market the Program

Run Public Service Announcements on the radio.

Step 6: Gather Materials

Prepare any notes you will need to discuss the book. Notify the purchasing department of each book selection to ensure that the books will be on hand at the library.

Book List

Colombo, George W. and Curtis Franklin. 2006. *Absolute Beginner's Guide to Podcasting*. Indianapolis: QUE.

Einstein, Mara. 2004. *Media Diversity: Economics, Ownership, and the FCC*. Mahwah, NJ: Lawrence Erlbaum.

Fedunkiw, Marianne. 2007. *Inventing the Radio*. New York: Crabtree.

Field, Shelly. 2004. *Career Opportunities in Radio*. New York: Checkmark Books/ Ferguson.

Haley, Connie K., Lynne A. Jacobsen, and Shai Robkin. 2007. *Radio Frequency Identification Handbook for Librarians*. Westport, CT: Libraries Unlimited.

Jones, Tarsha Nicole. 2007. *Have You Met Miss Jones? The Life and Loves of Radio's Most Controversial Diva*. New York: One World/Ballantine.

Krieg, Joyce. 2005. *Riding Gain: A Talk Radio Mystery*. New York: St. Martin's Minotaur/ Thomas Dunne Books.

Lieberman, Philip A. 1996. *Radio's Morning Show Personalities: Early Hour Broadcasters and Deejays from the 1920s to the 1990s*. Jefferson, NC: McFarland & Co.

Mitchell, Jack W. 2005. *Listener Supported: The Culture and History of Public Radio*. Westport, CT: Praeger.

Phillips, Lisa A. 2006. *Public Radio: Behind the Voices*. New York: CDS Books.

Reeves, Diane Lindsey, Gail Karlitz, and Don Rauf. 2005. *Career Ideas for Teens in the Arts and Communications*. New York: Ferguson.

Rolls, Albert. 2006. *New Media*. Bronx, NY: H.W. Wilson.

Saulsberry, Rodney. 2007. *Step Up to the Mic: A Positive Approach to Succeeding in Voice-Overs*. Agoura Hills, CA: Tomdor.

Smiley, Tavis and David Ritz. 2006. *What I Know for Sure: My Story of Growing Up in America*. New York: Anchor Books.

Taylor, T. Allan and James Robert Parish. 2007. *Career Opportunities in the Internet, Video Games, and Multimedia*. New York: Checkmark Books.

Step 7: Set Up the Program Area

Set up the room for the radio show in an arrangement that is conducive to discussion and easy microphone access for everyone.

Step 8: Conduct the Event

The talk show host guides the program, interviewing the other radio guests about various topics and concerns, and then leading a discussion of the book with the librarian. The discussion can be about the author as well as the book, and the other guests may join in the discussion. Callers are welcome to call in and comment on the book. The title of the book to be discussed the next quarter is announced. Readers are encouraged to go to the library to find the book for the next program. During each broadcast a library staff member offers helpful information such as how to get a library card and announces upcoming events.

Step 9: Evaluate the Program

Evaluations are helpful for planning future programs. To get suggestions for future shows, and to help publicize the program, place numerous copies of the Radio Listener Questionnaire (see Figure 24.1) at the library check-out desks.

Figure 24.1. Word-Up Radio Listener Questionnaire

Word-Up Radio Listener Questionnaire

The purpose of the radio show is to promote the <CITY> to teens and to increase library usage and awareness.

1. Do you listen to the radio on Sunday mornings?   Yes / No

2. Have you ever listened to <RADIO PROGRAM> on <RADIO STATION> at <TIME>?   Yes / No

3. Have you heard Word-Up, the quarterly book discussion?   Yes / No

4. Did you enjoy the program?   Yes / No

5. Would you like to hear more programs like this?   Yes / No

6. Did this program entice you to visit and/or check something out at the library?   Yes / No

7. Will you be using the library's many resources in the future?   Yes / No

8. Are you planning to listen to our next production of Word-Up on <RADIO STATION> at <TIME>?   Yes / No

9. Will you tell a friend?   Yes / No

Suggestions for future book discussions:

_____

_____

_____

General comments:

_____

_____

_____

Please check one:

_____ Youth   _____ Teen   _____ Adult

Thank You!

25
VIRTUAL TOURS
(IN-SERVICE TRAINING
FOR SCHOOL TEACHERS)

PROGRAM DESCRIPTION

Teachers can earn continuing professional education credits certified by the school district by attending an in-service training at the library. The librarians give the teachers five- to ten-minute orientations of the many resources available to them in each department. The orientation is followed by a Library Scavenger Hunt.

PROGRAM GOALS

This program will support collaboration and cooperation between schools and the library. Working together, libraries and schools can provide coordinated programs and activities to bring students and books together that will focus on family reading and foster a literate community environment. The presentations from each department of the library will give the teachers much more information than they would know to ask about on an individual visit to the library. If libraries REACH the teachers, they will TEACH the students, giving them opportunities to build many of the developmental assets.

HOW TO DO IT

Step 1: Make a Plan

This program is planned to motivate schoolteachers to come to the library by offering something that every teacher wants and needs—continuing education credits. Contact the local school district and arrange a meeting with the school district superintendents or the curriculum directors and the library administration. Plan to show the PowerPoint presentation on the accompanying CD (and shown in Figure 25.1) to present the program idea and to initiate discussion. Discuss the time and content of the in-service day so the school administration can determine the continuing education credits to offer. Decide which grade level and subject areas the in-service session will focus on. The schools will contact the teachers the program will benefit. This workshop can be customized to reach any special group of teachers, such as English teachers, science teachers, elementary and middle school teachers, and so forth.

During the program, a representative from each library department gives a short orientation on what that department has to offer the students and teachers. Ask staff from the following departments to participate: business and periodicals, humanities and information,

Figure 25.1. Teacher In-Service Training PowerPoint Presentation

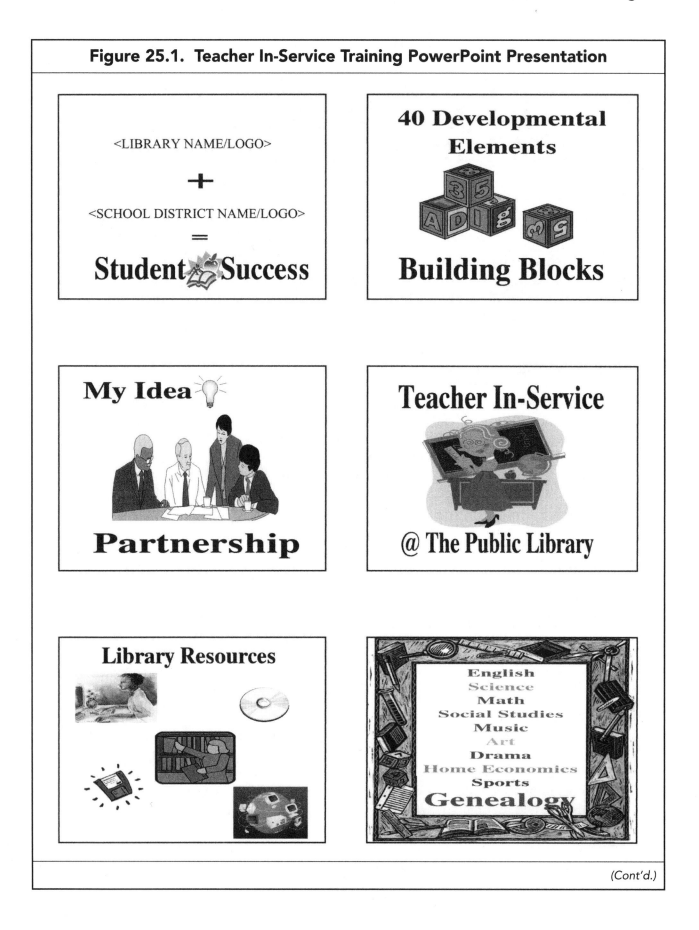

(Cont'd.)

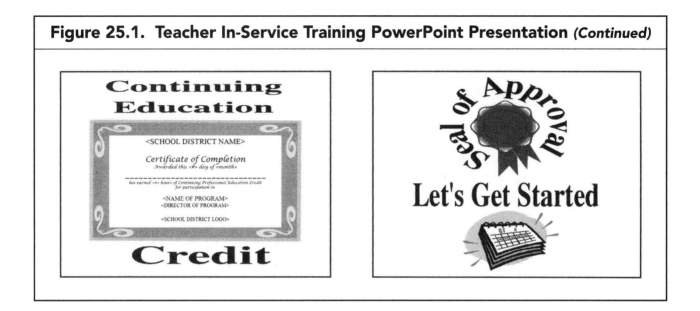

Figure 25.1. Teacher In-Service Training PowerPoint Presentation *(Continued)*

genealogy, media, children/youth, outreach, interlibrary loan, and circulation. Ask a representative to speak on behalf of all library branches. A question-and-answer session follows each presentation. A Library Scavenger Hunt with prizes or a task assignment required by the school will reinforce the new information. Arrange for incentives for the Scavenger Hunt.

Step 2: Set a Date, Book a Space

Schedule the program to coordinate with the school's scheduled in-service day. Coordinate the time of day with the school administrators.

The in-service training needs a lecture-style set-up in a meeting room or lecture hall with a presentation area for the librarians. The Scavenger Hunt will take place throughout the library.

Step 3: Book the Presenter

Ask representatives of each department in your library to prepare a five- to ten-minute informative orientation about their departments. They should focus on the materials and services they offer for the subject areas and age levels of the students the attending teachers have.

Step 4: Create a Program Format and Agenda

- Keynote speaker supplied by the school district
- Orientation presentations by library staff
- Library Scavenger Hunt

Step 5: Market the Program

The school district sends notices to the teachers and prospective participants about the in-service training and the continuing education credits.

Step 6: Gather Materials

Ask all service desk staff to prepare at least two questions about their departments for the Scavenger Hunt. Compile the questions and make copies for each teacher. Notify all service desk staff to have their information materials ready for the Library Scavenger Hunt (see Figure 25.2).

Book List

Forte, Imogene. 1989. *Teacher-Tested Timesavers*. Nashville, TN: Incentive Publications, Inc.

Gildner, Carol. 2001. *Enjoy Teaching: Helpful Hints for the Classroom*. Lanham, MD: Scarecrow Education.

Gordon, Thomas and Noël Burch. 1974. *T.E.T.: Teacher Effectiveness Training*. New York: P. H. Wyden.

Kelley, W. Michael. 2003. *Rookie Teaching for Dummies*. New York: Wiley.

Kosty, Carlita. 2002. *History Fair Workbook: A Manual for Teachers, Students, and Parents*. Lanham, MD: Scarecrow Press.

Macmillan/McGraw-Hill. 1993. *A to Z Handbook: Staff Development Guide*. New York: Macmillan/McGraw-Hill School.

McClaine, L.S. 1997. *Games for Learning: A Curriculum Supplement for Homeschoolers*. Moscow, ID: Nutmeg Publications.

Partin, Ronald L. 2005. *Classroom Teacher's Survival Guide: Practical Strategies, Management Techniques, and Reproducibles for New and Experienced Teachers*. San Francisco: Jossey-Bass.

Silverman, Marvin. 1989. *Teacher Survival Training*. Hollywood, FL: Affiliates for Evaluation & Therapy.

Simpson, Martha Seif and Lucretia I. Duwel. 2007. *Bringing Classes into the Public Library: A Handbook for Librarians*. Jefferson, NC: McFarland & Co.

Springer, Steve, Brandy Alexander, and Kimberly Persiani-Becker. 2007. *The Creative Teacher: An Encyclopedia of Ideas to Energize Your Curriculum*. New York: McGraw-Hill.

Thompson, Julia G. 2007. *The First-Year Teacher's Survival Guide: Ready-to-Use Strategies, Tools & Activities for Meeting the Challenges of Each School Day*. San Francisco: Jossey-Bass.

Warner, Jack, Clyde Bryan, and Diane Warner. 2006. *The Unauthorized Teacher's Survival Guide: An Essential Reference for Both New and Experienced Educators!* Indianapolis: JIST Works.

Step 7: Set Up the Program Area

Set up the meeting room in a lecture-style configuration.

Step 8: Conduct the Event

- The teachers assemble in the lecture area.
- The keynote speaker, provided by the school district, speaks.
- Each service desk representative gives a five-minute orientation of his or her area, including the location, the resources in the area, and how to access the materials. The orientations should be customized to the audience. For example, if the audience is composed of science teachers, how can each department help them and their students?

**Figure 25.2. Library Scavenger Hunt Instructions
for Teacher In-Service Training**

Library Scavenger Hunt Instructions
for Teacher In-Service Training

<LIBRARY LOGO>

LIBRARY SCAVENGER HUNT
For Teachers

Name:	Phone #:
School:	Work Phone #:
Subject:	Grade(s) Taught:
E-mail:	

Rules: There are ten questions that will take you into all parts of the library. You do not have to work on the questions in order. You may work independently or in groups. You have 30 minutes to complete all ten questions. Please return to the Lecture Hall when done to receive a gift.

The first to complete the hunt will receive a prize! Good luck!

1. List two newspapers from areas outside the <CITY> area.

    (1) _____ (2) _____

2. Find books on college entrance tests such as the SAT or ACT. List the titles and call numbers of two books in the area.

    (1) _____ (2) _____

3. Locate the New Book Section. Name the title and author of a book that interests you.

    Title _____

    Author _____

(Cont'd.)

**Figure 25.2. Library Scavenger Hunt Instructions
for Teacher In-Service Training (Continued)**

4. Find a PAC terminal (online catalog). List three ways of researching an item.

   a. _____

   b. _____

   c. _____

5. Browse through the fiction section. Find a book by an author whose last name starts with the same letter as your last name.

   Book Title _____

Author's last name	Your last name
_____	_____

6. In the newly organized Spanish section give the title and author of one book.

   Book Title _____

   Author _____

7. In the Genealogy section find a high school annual; give the name of the school and the yearbook name.

   _____   _____

8. Locate the teen center. What is the theme of the decorations on the wall in that area?

   _____

9. Go to the youth center. Find the toy collection. Name two of the toys on display.

   (1) _____   (2) _____

10. Find the Media Department. Jot down the title of an audio book, a DVD, and a video that interest you.

   Audio Book: Title _____

   DVD: Title _____

   Video: Title _____

- Teachers are allowed to ask questions and make comments.
- Teachers are encouraged to visit any area of interest to complete a task assigned by their organization or to complete the Library Scavenger Hunt.

Step 9: Evaluate the Program

Evaluations are helpful for planning future programs. Customize the evaluation form from Part I (see Figure I.3 on CD) for participants to fill out. Collect the forms as the audience leaves.

PART III

THE FINISH LINE

CONCLUSION

Everywhere I go I meet librarians looking for a way to reach young people. We continue to reach out to teens in an effort to promote education, self-expression, and self-esteem. Schools and public libraries are all in the same business, helping students to succeed in life. Working together, we can provide opportunities for teens to build the 40 Developmental Assets®, which are the building blocks that help young people grow up healthy, caring, and responsible.

As a result of the teen programming held at the Fort Worth Public Library, over 95 percent of the teens active on the Teen Advisory Board (TAB) have gone on to some form of higher education after high school. The majority continued on to college. Many teens have chosen a career path based on certain programs offered at the library.

- The first TAB president, who often represented the library at many speaking engagements, attended college to become a radio and television announcer. Because of his leadership abilities, he also became a leader in college, serving as the student body president for two years. He will graduate in the spring of 2009.
- Another member decided to major in communications at Texas Christian University because of the interviewing skills she gained while participating as one of the hosts of the teen cable show "Check It Out @ the Library." She is a senior at this time, with plans of hosting her own television show upon graduation.
- Still another member, after being involved with many the of the music productions held at the library, has formed a professional jazz group of his own called State of Mind, in which he plays an outstanding saxophone. He is now in college with a double major, engineering and, yes, music.
- The other day I ran into another former TAB president working at a retail store. She is also attending college, majoring in dance and business with hopes of one day having her own dance studio.
- Yet another former member, who frequently presented book reviews for the teen cable show, is in the process of writing his own book.

In the library a few summers ago I met a couple of youth from Seattle, Washington, visiting their grandmother for the summer. I invited them to join the TAB while they were in town. The board welcomed them with open arms, and they became actively involved and participated in the different events, programs, and field trips. A few months after they had gone home to Seattle, their grandmother stopped in to tell me thanks. She said that she had received a call from her daughter, their mother, in Washington asking what she had done to her two children. Her daughter said that they had come back changed. The younger boy, who had always made good grades, even without studying hard, never brought a book home before. He was now more conscientious about his assignments and actually brought homework home. The mother noticed he was taking more pride in his work. The older sister, a junior in high school at the time, began researching for scholarships and applying for colleges. When asked why was she starting so soon she answered, "Ms. Jones said we should start now, because it's never too soon to start preparing for our future." The grandmother said the children told her that it had been the best summer they ever had. And they spent it at the library.

These are but a few examples of the positive outcome of programming for teens. It is apparent, through discussions with fellow librarians and library personnel, that there is a great need for a book that will teach the "how to" of planning and implementing successful teen programming. *Start-to-Finish YA Programs* is the book to fulfill this need. This book will help you to think outside the box. It gives you a starting point from which to create new and exciting programs of your own. I encourage you to look at each program packet and make it your own. If you work in a small library, reduce the program to fit your size. On the other hand, if you work in a large library, expand the program to suit your needs. Get young people actively involved. Ask their opinion on how they would like to see the program work. Believe me, you will get a response. And it will be creative and innovative, and the teens will take ownership in the activity.

Now we have covered the basics in "Let's Get Started"; we have charted your course with 25 practical ready-to-use programs with samples and examples; and we have taken you to the finish line, the outcome of programming for teens. The only thing left for you to do is to begin your teen program. *Start-to-Finish YA Programs* will show you how to get started and take you all the way through the finish line. Remember, you can change a life, helping teens to grow up to be healthy, caring, and responsible adults, one program at a time. If you are ready to start making a difference in the lives of young people, raise your right hand and say these words out loud: "IF IT IS TO BE, IT IS UP TO ME."

GRANT-WRITING RESOURCES

The following books and Web sites can make the grant-writing process easier.

Books

Browning, Beverly A. 2005. *Grant Writing for Dummies*. New York: Wiley.
Carlson, Mim. 2002. *Winning Grants: Step by Step*, 2nd ed. San Francisco: Jossey-Bass.
Karsh, Ellen and Arlen Sue Fox. 2003. *The Only Grant-Writing Book You'll Ever Need: Top Grant Writers and Grant Givers Share Their Secrets*. New York: Avalon
Thompson, Waddy. 2007. *The Complete Idiot's Guide to Grant Writing*, 2nd ed. Royersford, PA: Alpha.

Web Sites

Basic Elements of Grant Writing
www.cpb.org/grants/grantwriting.html: Guideposts to help you through the grant-writing process from the Corporation for Public Broadcasting

Library Fund-Raising and Grant Writing
www.librarysupportstaff.com/find$.html: School grants—your one-stop site for PK–12 grant opportunities and grant-writing resources

School Grants: Grant Writing Tips

www.schoolgrants.org/grant_tips.htm: Tips for writing school grants, with links to other resources

www.schoolgrants.org/schoolgrants2/links/grant_writing.htm: SG links to grant-writing resources

Writing a Successful Grant Proposal

www.mcf.org/mcf/grant/writing.htm: Information for grant writing in Minnesota that can be used by anyone

Sources of Grants

Foundations On-Line, "Foundations & Grantmakers Directory." Available at: www.foundations .org/grantmakers.html.

Classroom Connection grants: http://classroomconnection.org.

"The Big Deal Book of Technology for K–12 Educators." Available at: www.bigdeal book.com/. A sourcebook of material of grants, contests, and awards

Miscellaneous Resources

License plate grants: Check with your superintendent's office.

Local businesses: Target, Wal-Mart, Dollar General, and McDonald's have grants.

Local foundations: Many communities have an educational or philanthropic foundation that awards grants.

ADDITIONAL RESOURCES

Avery, Elizabeth Fuseler, Terry Dahlin, and Deborah A. Carver. 2001. *Staff Development: A Practical Guide*, 3rd ed. Chicago: American Library Association.

Field, Selma and Edwin Field. 1993. *Publicity Manual for Libraries: A Professional Guide to Communicating with the Community*. British Columbia: Knowledge Network Press.

Jones, Patrick. 1995. "Against All Odds: Creating Support for Serving Young Adults in Public Libraries." *Journal of Youth Services in Libraries* 8, no. 3 (Spring): 233–242.

Jones, Patrick. 2002. *New Directions for Library Service to Young Adults*. Chicago: American Library Association.

Karp, Rashelle S. 2002. *Powerful Public Relations: A How-to Guide for Libraries*. Chicago: American Library Association.

Lundberg, Carol. 2001. *The Effects of Time-Limitations and Peer Relationship on Adult Student Learning: A Causal Model*. Presented at the 2001 Association for the Study of Higher Education Annual Conference. Richmond, Virginia, November 15–18.

Maniace, Len. 2003. "Economy Taking Toll on Libraries." *The Journal News*, February 6. Available at: www.nyjournalnews.com/newsroom/020603/b0106librarywoes.html.

Meskauskas, Debora. 2002. "Planning Special Events." In *Powerful Public Relations: A How-to Guide for Libraries*, edited by Rashelle S. Karp. Chicago: American Library Association.

Sherman, Steve. 1992. *ABC's of Library Promotion*, 3rd ed. Metuchen, NJ: Scarecrow Press.

Simerly, Robert. 1990. *Planning and Marketing Conferences and Workshops: Tips, Tools, and Techniques*. San Francisco: Jossey-Bass.

Swigger, Keith. 1995. "A Research Agenda for YALSA." *Journal of Youth Services in Libraries* 8, no. 3 (Spring): 267–272.

Turner, Anne. 2000. *Vote Yes for Libraries: A Guide to Winning Ballot Measure Campaigns for Library Funding*. Jefferson, NC: McFarland & Co.

Wheeler, Joseph L. 1924. *The Library and the Community*. Chicago: American Library Association.

INDEX

Page numbers followed by "f" indicate figures.

ABOUT THE AUTHOR

Ella W. Jones, a Librarian/Teen Specialist and new author, is going full-speed ahead! She's partnering with dozens of community organizations and setting new trends in adult and teen services. Previously, Ella was "the best-kept secret" at the Fort Worth Public Library, but that has all changed.

Ella holds three master's degrees: Education, Counseling & Guidance, and Library Science. She has spent more than 20 years educating students. In 1976, she was recognized as Educator of the Year, while teaching high school in Fort Wayne, Indiana. After arriving in Texas, Ella became employed by Procter & Gamble Distribution Company and received several merit awards, such as Dallas Elite Winner and Unit Shipment Champion 1985. Returning to education in Arlington, Texas, she earned the title of Secondary Teacher of the Year in 1994. Of all her accomplishments, Ella is most proud of having a scholarship named in her honor in 2004: the Ella W. Jones Creative Arts Award, presented by students of South Side High School (in Fort Wayne, Indiana) where she had taught almost 25 years earlier. That same year in May, Ella received the Director's Gold Star Award "For extraordinary efforts in bringing groups and individuals to the Fort Worth Public Library and for high level of visibility in the community." She was selected as a "Tall Texan" by the Texas Library Association in 2006, one of the highest compliments a Texas librarian can receive. In 2007, Ella was nominated for the "Distinguished Student Award" by the Library and Information Science faculty of North Texas University, one of several of her college alma maters.

Ella has presented outstanding workshops for North Texas Regional Library Systems (NTRLS), such as "Can We Talk: About Teen Programming?," a workshop designed for urban libraries, and "Can We Talk a Little Closer?," a workshop for small and rural libraries. Both workshops were simulcast. Ella, along with Osei Baffour, a Fort Worth Public Library administrator, has presented programs for the Texas Library Association (TLA) annual conferences, "Teens R Us" (2005) and "No Patron Left Behind" (2006). In 2007, Ella presented a new program for the TLA conference titled "Strengthening Communities with C.L.A.S.S.: Connecting Libraries and Schools Strategically." And in 2008, Ella presented "No Patron Left Behind" alone for NTRLS.

Ella has used her educational and sales background to produce knockout programming which included an annual Hip-Hop Symposium that drew hundreds of students, record label executives, and aspiring artists. While working for Fort Worth Public Library, Ella established a very active and highly respected Teen Advisory Board, and she also served as the executive producer of the teen cable show *Check It Out @ the Library*, which she created. Currently Ella has returned once again to her first love, education, and is now the Code Compliance/ Executive Officer for Man In The Mirror, a tutoring and test preparation organization.